TO Finish Well

MARJIE SUTTON

Clearing the decks to make space for life!

Copyright © 2022 Marjie Sutton

Self Help / Personal Finances / Death & Bereavement

All Rights Reserved. No part of this book may be reproduced in any manner whatsoever, or stored in any information storage system, or transmitted in any form or by any means, electronic, mechanical, photocopying, recording, or otherwise, without the prior written consent of the publisher, except in the case of brief quotations with proper reference, embodied in articles and reviews.

Unless otherwise indicated, all Scripture quotations are taken from the Holy Bible, New Living Translation, copyright © 1996, 2004, 2015 by Tyndale House Foundation. Used by permission of Tyndale House Publishers, Carol Stream, Illinois 60188, USA. All rights reserved.

Printed in the United Kingdom

ISBN: 978-1-3999-3752-8

Published by: Living to Finish Well

Illustrations by: Irina Stepanova and Rebecca Roberts

Editorial Production: The Editor's Chair

ACKNOWLEDGMENTS

What I thought would be a walk in the park became something of a marathon. Putting together some helpful pointers for my nearest and dearest to 'get their affairs in order' led me to delving into deeper questions than I had imagined, and holding myself to account for streamlining my own life!

I am grateful for all who have encouraged and helped me on this journey, whether you realised it or not.

Firstly, a big thanks to my wonderful extended family; unknowingly, you were the inspiration for the book in the first place! Thank you for your encouragement and support – especially those who have already taken action in response! The finished product is my gift to you all. In particular, a big thank you to Simon, Jon and Kate Kensington for the time and support you've given to the LTFW project already. You are a great blessing!

This book would never have reached publication by my efforts alone and I am grateful for the team that joined me, using their professional expertise to bring it to birth. Huge thanks to all of you...

...Denise Roberts and her team at the Editor's Chair for your whole-hearted support, patience, guidance and professionalism.

Special thanks to Irina Stepanova and Rebecca Roberts for your help with the illustrations.

Simon and Jon Kensington and Richard Merritt – what a total joy to work with you all and see your amazing gifts and professional expertise in action. Si – your steering of the design process has been inspiring. Thank you for tuning in, teasing out and interpreting my thoughts so brilliantly. Jonny – you've walked with me on this journey probably longer than anyone, the best sounding board ever. Your patience, kindness and creativity have played a bigger part in keeping me going than you realise. I am in awe of your many talents and look forward to working together developing resources. Richard – your enthusiasm and 'can do' attitude have been a breath of fresh air in the final stretch towards publication.

Huge thanks, too, to my many friends who have been aware of 'the book' and supported/prayed me through it all, in particular, Mhairi Esposito, Brigitte Gobbe and Lee Ann Thompson. Thank you for listening the many times I've rambled on, for your wise responses and for keeping me going when I've felt like giving up.

My thanks to Andy Knox, Tony Summers and John Morris for your support and willingness to recommend the book. As professionals who help people navigate key aspects of life, your endorsements mean a lot. Also to Andy for allowing me to use your videos on forgiveness. I'm grateful for your generosity and unquestioning support.

Above all I am so grateful to my amazing Father God for His unchanging love and faithfulness throughout my life. If I have anything worth sharing it is all thanks to Him.

RECOMMENDATIONS

Death is never an easy thing to talk about. But it is an inevitable part of life. Pretending or hoping it will miss us out, somehow, can leave all kinds of problems for those left behind. Sometimes it comes to us young and too quickly, sometimes when we are ripe in age. It can be unexpectedly sudden and cruel, gentle and silent, or can even feel unnecessarily prolonged.

For those of us who are left, not only is there the heartache and grief of having to learn to keep on living without the person who has gone, but often there are lots of practical things to sort out, which we were unprepared for. This book gets to the real nub of these issues. Pragmatic, yet compassionate, straight-talking yet kind, Marjie Sutton invites you to live well in the present, so you can know, whenever your death occurs, everything is prepared and you, yourself, are ready.

All of this is undergirded by Marjie's own faith in a God who loves us. You may not agree with her, but whatever you think about this and 'life after death', it's an important thing to consider, as you more realistically accept and embrace your own mortality. So, whether you need help in sorting out your finances, understanding the legal aspects, having tough conversations with your loved ones, or facing life's big questions – this little book contains pearls of wisdom you would do well to treasure.

Dr Andy Knox
Associate Medical Director for Lancashire and South Cumbria

I have had the privilege of knowing Marjie Sutton in a professional capacity for five years.

In that time, I have been impressed by the clarity and accuracy of insight Marjie brings to matters we need to address but don't want to confront. Her suggestions are always very helpful and her book, *Living to Finish Well*, is no exception. Many people will find Marjie's masterpiece both template and practical 'to do' list in one!

There is a well-known saying 'we all reap what we sow'. In *Living to Finish Well*, Marjie pulls back the curtain on the concept of cause and effect to help us understand the practical consequences of our actions or inaction in managing our financial and property affairs, as well as family relationships. She gets these challenging beasts on the table for us to carve up at our leisure. And carve them up we better had! For if we don't, by default we will have placed others in the driving seat.

I therefore have no hesitation in recommending *Living to Finish Well*. In fact, Marjie's book complements my firm's services so well we will provide it to both new and existing clients, as the opportunity presents.

Take it. Read it. Read it again. Make notes. Take the medicine. You will feel better.

John Morris DipFA MLIBF
Managing Director
The Harvest Partnership Ltd

Marjie Sutton, with her characteristically direct and uncompromising style, throws down the challenge to us all. Clearly drawing deeply on her own experiences at the same time as providing a wealth of practical advice, she pulls us all up short.

Living to Finish Well is thought-provoking, causing us to reflect not only on our own mortality but also the needs of those that will be left behind when we die. It conveys a very positive message. Rather than feeling helpless, there are simple (although not easy) steps that can be taken to face up to the taboos and difficult questions which we would rather leave to one side, but enable steps to be taken towards the healing of broken relationships.

As one starts to turn the pages it becomes very clear that the book is actually about living, not dying. It conveys a very powerful message about the way that life should be lived in the here and now.

When someone dies, family, friends, business partners and acquaintances not only face their own moment of mortality. Often, it is also the moment when relationships which have been built, sometimes over a lifetime, either rise to the challenge and become even stronger or, due to poor preparation or a lack of understanding, overwhelming emotions can just get too much. It is a time when there is a need for sensitivity as people are at their most vulnerable, and it can make or break a relationship in a way that no other major life event can.

Unresolved conflicts within families (and outside) can and do carry on for generations. Marjie takes us through the means that we have to help resolve those conflicts while we are still alive, rather than leaving them as part of our legacy to be perpetuated for the next generation and beyond.

As senior partner of a law firm for a few decades now, I have first-hand experience of this in action. I recall a will reading I undertook at the executor's request immediately after the funeral (rarely a good idea!). Within a few minutes half of the family had become extremely agitated, were clearly upset and walked out of the room. As far as I am aware, there has been no further communication between the two sides of the family (apart from through lawyers) since that day. If the deceased had read Marjie's book the outcome may have been different. One can only hope so.

On the whole people do great things with their lives, create amazing relationships with family, friends and colleagues and do their best to look after loved ones and the community and environment in which they live.

We owe it to those that we love to let them leave behind the legacy great people deserve – Marjie's book can only add to the chances of that becoming a reality.

Tony Summers
Senior Partner
Wellers Law Group

TABLE OF CONTENTS

Acknowledgments iii

Recommendations vii

1. CARPE DIEM 1
Seize the day

2. READY OR NOT 7
Time and tide wait for no man

3. WE NEED TO TALK 19
Essential conversations before it's too late

4. WHERE THERE'S A WILL 31
Getting to grips with essentials we'd rather ignore

5. THE YOUNG ONES ... .55
Caring for your greatest treasure

6. STAYING AHEAD OF THE GAME. 65
Prevention rather than cure

7. LIVING LIGHTLY 81
Clearing the decks to make space for life

8. DEALING WITH THE INEVITABLE 97
Finding treasure in unexpected places

9. TO INFINITY AND BEYOND! 113
Just when you thought it was all over

Appendix 121

About the Author 131

1 CARPE DIEM

Seize the day

"The secret of getting ahead is getting started."
—Mark Twain

The journey of this book began after the unexpected loss, within a handful of weeks, of two dear family members. I realised, with some concern, that a number (most?!) of the next generation of my family had not yet got around to sorting out matters such as making a will, let alone getting to grips with thorny questions, such as who would care for their minor children if something happened to them. With that realisation, I decided that, perhaps, it would be good to pull together some thoughts and information to help them, and many like them, take action.

What started as a focus on 'getting your affairs in order' quickly developed to addressing the journey of life towards its inevitable end. I recognised how bad many of us are at this. I thought I was going to write about finishing well, but before getting very far I realised that it's all about living well, which doesn't just mean being successful and having fun. I also saw that, far from just being a helpful handbook for the elderly or those who know their days are numbered, it's crucial for adults of all ages. So, whether you're a 20-something, or in your 90s, this is important stuff!

There's something about the idea of 'putting things in order' that creates resistance in some of us. We don't like to be told what to do, to feel that we're being controlled or regimented! However, bringing order into something actually results in peace. Where there was chaos, there's now peace because, whether we want to admit it or not, guilty feelings about things not yet done always lurk somewhere – however deeply buried – in our consciousness.

Hopefully, this book will provoke you to think about things differently, challenge attitudes and start a process that will help you to find peace. A process that will free you to be an amazing blessing to others, both those you love and even those you haven't given thought to in a long time. While trying to cover all aspects of having a life in order, it's not going to be a step-by-step handbook of what to do and how to do it, although it will include information and suggest some resources to point you in the right direction. My hope is that it will simply help you to focus on some of those things we all avoid, inspire you to seize the day, get everything in order and to, perhaps, begin living to a different rhythm.

We'll look at:

- Essential conversations and preparations; the things we leave undone to our potential peril
- Helpful preparations; putting things in good order so that executors have as easy a task as possible
- Thoughts and tips to ease the way for those responsible for dealing with someone else's affairs
- And finally, a section to challenge our thoughts and beliefs about 'what comes next'.

How to read the book

There will be an overlap between some of the chapters, where something touched on may have been covered in more detail in another chapter. With this in mind, you may find it helpful to use the journal pages to quickly note down the things that particularly speak to you as you read; issues that ring a bell and which you know need your deeper attention. To help with this process, each chapter concludes with questions and/or suggestions to get you thinking and help you work out your own plan of action.

There may be parts you can skip straight over – for example, if you can tick all the boxes outlined in chapters four to six. While they may be, to some, the most difficult and challenging, they're probably the most straightforward in real terms! Some themes covered may highlight key issues that need to be addressed that will take time, grace and courage, whereas others are simply talking about very straightforward and practical matters. I encourage you to read every chapter, even those where you feel you've got it all sussed; you might find there are still things to think about, or changes you need to make.

I suggest, too, that you read the whole book through, making notes as you go of the things that jump out at you. When you've finished it, review your notes, work out priorities and then go back to the beginning and work through it again methodically. You could well find, to your surprise, that you can actually multi-task, as some suggested actions are easily done in the course of everyday life, alongside those that may need some dedicated time and attention.

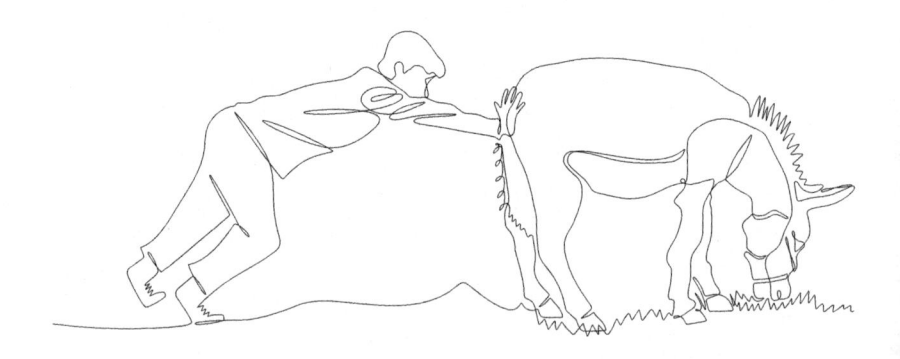

Disclaimer

Please note – any information in the book about legal matters, etc. relates specifically to the UK, so if you live elsewhere you will need to do your own investigation about what the law requires in your country. That applies also to the UK, as rules sometimes differ in each nation, particularly around wills, LPAs (Lasting Power of Attorney), etc. However, the subjects covered are important for everyone, wherever you live.

While I have taken every effort to check the validity of the facts about processes, these must be checked by you, the reader as, while they were correct at the time of writing, legislation changes and I can take no responsibility for their continuing validity.

2 READY OR NOT...

Time and tide wait for no man

> *"Preparing for death is one of the most empowering things you can do. Thinking about death clarifies your life."*
>
> —Candy Chang

It's interesting that many of us spend a lot of time and energy making plans for the future, often counting the days to a long-awaited event or goal. Yet this 'future' somehow fails to include the one known (albeit not usually eagerly-awaited) outcome – the conclusion of our time on this earth. Instead, we become masters of procrastination, relying on the premise that there's plenty of time to think about these things.

Finishing our lives well doesn't simply happen at the end, it has to have started way earlier. For some, death will come sharply, suddenly, shockingly, stealing away all the time we thought was securely ahead when we could 'get our affairs in order' and tie up loose ends. We thought it would be a day far ahead in the future for which we had plenty of time to prepare. For others, the end is slower, a path to be consciously walked when there may be time to prepare, but little energy or inclination to do so. After all, who wants to spend precious and limited time dealing with tedious administration when we just want to enjoy the time left with those we love, or finishing off beloved, yet neglected projects; let alone getting to that elusive 'bucket list'?

Finishing well is, in essence, all about living well. It's not about morbidly focusing on death, nor simply making sure those 'affairs' are in order. It's about living in a rhythm and structure that creates peace of mind, harmony and blessing to all, and adds in the bonus of knowing that the ones eventually doing our tidying up will have a smooth path.

As I noted in the introduction, when I set out on this journey I thought I would be talking about all those important practical things that are dangerously left undone. Having just suffered a family loss, I became acutely aware that many of my family and friends had not yet even made a will, let alone taken action regarding key issues. Issues such as what would happen to their children if they were to die, or even to themselves if suddenly they lost the ability to manage their own affairs.

With these thoughts in mind, I began writing, hoping to challenge some behaviours, dispel a few myths (dare I say, superstitions?!) and encourage people to stop procrastinating, grasp the nettle and get their 'affairs' well and truly in order. It's tough for those left with the responsibility of managing things after our death when they're often in the throes of grief, especially as so much has to be done without undue delay. How much worse this becomes if our affairs are in chaos. Surely we owe it to those we love to leave things in as good order as possible, so that everything necessary can be completed as easily as possible? Come on, this makes sense from every angle!

As soon as I began to write, I realised that I was talking about so much more than 'finishing well'. It's not simply about ensuring that at the end of life you can leave a legacy of money or possessions to those you love and care about. It's also about living well, freely and lightly, uncluttered by all those things/tasks/issues that are stuffed into the cupboards and drawers of our thoughts and conscience. Some of these stay hidden until discovered by the poor, unsuspecting person with the task of sorting everything out and some, at times, burst out of their confinement spreading chaos and mess at our own feet.

By 'living lightly', I don't mean living in denial, pretending everything is fine and that nothing needs to be done. On the contrary, it's considering how we can order our lives so that we don't get caught off guard, finding ourselves in a situation where it's too late. That horrible place where all the 'if only's' suddenly become our reality, where we find ourselves living in 'should have, could have'... but now we can't. Living in a season of sorrow and grief is one thing; finding ourselves living in regret is quite another, putting us under the hand of a hard taskmaster, one from which we struggle to be free and probably never succeed. Even if we manage to bury something deep, it's always there.

I can't emphasise enough how important it is to think about these things now, whatever your age. You may not be old in years, but do you, for example, have children under 18? If something happened to you, what would be the effect on your family, nuclear or extended? What about the one(s) left to deal with your estate; would it be plain sailing or would they be walking into chaos?

It's about so much more than paperwork. It's about relationships, about learning to share our hearts, to be totally un-British and tell people we love them and what we value in them. It's not simply sorting out who gets what, but creating legacies that can't be measured. It's about downloading wisdom, what we've learned that may equip the next generation to go deeper and further than us. It's about enjoying life to the full and making good memories with those we love the most that will bring comfort and joy when we're no longer around, adding narrative that will become part of treasured family history and traditions. It's spending time with those we love, just 'being', hanging out, sharing memories, chewing over big questions and decisions, chilling and having fun. Having the type of relationships where we can talk about anything in the confidence of loving and being loved, just as we are. It's keeping our lives in good order, as we will unpack in the following pages.

In the final analysis, it is, of course, all about love! So, why do we put it off?

Probably the most common reason is our conviction that there's plenty of time. 'It's on my to-do list, but I'm only 20/30-something so there's no need to rush'. Sometimes, there's a hidden fear, almost a superstition: 'If I write my will, I'll probably die!' Yes, you're not the only one who thinks that somehow this exercise will tempt fate and that will be that. Maybe working out what to do and who to ask is challenging, so we join the ostrich with our head buried in the sand, hoping that if we ignore it long enough it will go away. That *will*, inevitably, be the case – or rather, we'll be the one going away and leaving mayhem for our nearest and dearest to handle. And try as you might, it's impossible to control and orchestrate things once you're no longer around! You meant for your favourite ring (or whatever) to go to a certain person and someone else has taken it instead, because you never got around to specifying your wishes. 'Noooo!' Sorry, it's too late.

So, how can we tackle the big questions of life and death in a way that shapes and forms our living, rather than thinking about them only when and if we're forced to do so by circumstances? As already noted, we don't know how long we've got on this earth. How do we regard life? Is it something to be grabbed by the throat, lived to the full, thinking only of today? Or is there more? I believe that life is eternal (although some may find this hard to grasp) and that the part lived out on earth affects all the rest, which is there for all who choose to trust in Jesus and follow Him. What if you don't have that belief? How can one find the courage to face death as a reality? The questions we may face when forced to think about them are relevant now, but we too often shelve them because we don't have a sense of urgency, or it's just too hard. Perhaps it may mean that we need to change and we don't want to, just yet.

While your will deals with the main aspects of whatever assets you have to pass on (which is for another chapter), there's far more to consider. Let's look at the legacy you'll leave behind beyond money, property and possessions.

Think of the things you've reflected on after losing someone you love; the regrets over the things you never talked about, the questions you always meant to ask but didn't, the things you always meant to do or places you wanted to visit together, but didn't get around to it. Perhaps saddest of all, the things you wish you'd said or done. Do you really want to risk leaving it until it's too late?

When you think about this, we're not only talking about tidying up our affairs and leaving everything in good shape for our executors. We're talking about living in a 'now' where we never miss the opportunity to tell someone we love them and what we love about them; where we are quick to heal hurts and fix breaches, making peace and bringing resolution to old wounds; where we make time for one another even when it's sacrificial; where we live in a way that brings life, joy and peace far beyond the boundaries of our own little (or big!) family. How much richer our lives would be if we could learn to live in a way that never leaves us with regrets because now 'it's too late'.

Some people live their whole lives holding on to offence, some of which wasn't even initially to do with them, grudges and feuds passed down a family line. These become more entrenched generation by generation, held on to with anger, bitterness, hatred and unforgiveness by those who weren't involved in the original fallout and probably don't have a clue what really happened. Whether this is the case, or we actually know the facts in great detail, there's well-documented evidence that, when we hold on to unforgiveness, we are the ones who suffer, far more than the one(s) who were the cause of our disaffection. Holding on to wounds, offences and grudges is toxic first and foremost to us. Is that a legacy we want to keep alive, to pass on to the next generation? Learning to forgive (which, by the way, involves acknowledging in your own mind and heart that there totally *is* something to forgive) brings such peace and restoration, whether or not the other party cares. More on this in Chapter Three.

There's much to think about, but don't get overwhelmed! There's also much to enjoy, whether it's people, places or pastimes. Whatever we put in there, we need to live life to the full, enjoying it here and now. It's important to have purpose, to order our lives well and have work that we enjoy. It's also important to live life with a full heart, making and taking opportunities – both planned and spontaneous – with those we love and also making new friends as we go.

Don't procrastinate any longer! It's time to get to work. Dealing with the nitty-gritty to get our affairs into good shape may seem tedious, but it brings its own reward, not least peace of mind. You may be surprised to discover that it's as much a part of living life with a capital 'L' as all the fun things. Both leave legacies and whether they're good or bad is in our hands.

To think about

- Why haven't I taken action? What's holding me back?
- How well organised do I think I am? If I die tonight, will I be leaving smooth waters or choppy seas? Plain sailing or carnage?
- How intentionally do I live each day, especially concerning relationships?
- What have I reflected on when losing someone I love – what do I most treasure about my memories of them? What would I like to be remembered for? What is the legacy I'm leaving?
- What are the memories, family traditions and history that I want to pass on? Are there things I *don't* want to pass on – hurts, offences, etc.?
- What have I been putting off that I need to deal with? Practical affairs, relationships, experiences…?
- Who do I need to spend time with, to deepen our relationship?
- What things are on my bucket list and when will I start doing them?

NOTES FROM THIS CHAPTER

MARJIE SUTTON

3 WE NEED TO TALK

Essential conversations before it's too late

"The time has come," the walrus said, "to talk of many things: of shoes and ships – and sealing wax – of cabbages and kings."
—Lewis Carroll

Probably one of the most difficult and awkward things for many of us is to talk about those things everyone wants to pretend don't exist. This can range from our wishes in the case of medical emergencies, to care when we're old, what songs we want at our funeral, whether we want to be buried or cremated, as well as all those 'what if' questions ... the list goes on!

We've already talked about our propensity to bury our heads in the sand when it comes to depressing or tough subjects and hopefully, you've come to see that facing the realities of living and dying doesn't have to cast a permanent shadow of misery over you. Getting your affairs in order early on *doesn't* mean that you'll probably die tomorrow. Far from it! Knowing that everything is in good order and can be easily accessed, understood and managed by whoever that falls to is liberating. It takes a weight off!

Let's pick up where we left off in the last chapter and think further about how we live in relationships with others. This may seem to be a strange thing to include in a chapter on 'essential conversations', but these things really are fundamental and deserving of close attention. Refusing to let offence – in whatever shape or form – live in your heart and mind frees you in the most amazing way. It really *is* true that dealing with things, choosing to forgive others and ourselves, sets us free, while refusing to forgive, but instead holding on to grudges, in reality keeps *us* in prison, rather than those we feel offended by.

At this point, you might need to take time to reflect on your relationships, past and present. Take an inventory, if you like, and honestly acknowledge to yourself where there are wounds or regrets that are as yet unhealed. Begin to work on them. This takes courage; most of us find it difficult to admit we may have been (or definitely were) wrong. At other times, we may have been the innocent party. We can kid ourselves that it doesn't matter now – too much water under the bridge and well, we're okay, aren't we? Maybe. Perhaps you've reached a level of acceptance you can live with, but the truth is that these 'skeletons in the cupboard' always prevent true freedom.

So, please, take the time for an honest, radical overhaul; use the journal pages to note the things that come to mind. If there's an issue of forgiveness and healing is needed, then find the courage to face it and act. It may be that the other party won't or can't respond, or won't be reconciled. Don't let that stop you. The truth is that choosing to forgive and/or ask for forgiveness releases YOU, whether it's reciprocated or not. And which of us really wants to live with a well of bitterness, anger and pain inside us when we can be free? It's never too late; even if the other person has since died, or we've completely lost contact with them, honestly facing the issue and speaking out forgiveness still brings release and healing.

While we're thinking about this huge subject, don't ever say, 'It doesn't matter'. I'm sure we can all recall situations where we have either been on the receiving end of hurt, or have caused it to someone else. Acknowledging that and asking for forgiveness takes courage, and so often 'Oh it's fine, it doesn't matter' is the kind of response we make or receive because it's awkward. But it *does* matter and it is important to acknowledge the wrong and speak words of forgiveness. When we just brush it aside because we're embarrassed, somehow the issue isn't put to rest, but compounded.

What about those 'inherited grudges' – the historic things that have come down through our family history? Do we want to perpetuate those and all that comes with them, or have we the courage to say, 'This far and no further', to stand in the gap and deal with it once and for all, releasing the shackles of unforgiveness from ourselves and our children? It may not be an easy thing to do, but the results are priceless as the weight of carrying offence and unforgiveness falls away, leaving us and our children with head and heart space free, rather than taken up with things way beyond our control.

This is such a broad and deep subject. What, you may ask, about those things that seem unforgivable – traumas, injustice, things that could be described as unbelievably evil? There is no quick and easy solution and such cases may require a longer journey and professional help. Whatever your situation may be, the key is acknowledging the pain and finding the courage to take that first step.

So, how and where can we begin? There are many books and other resources available. My good friend, Dr Andy Knox, has made a couple of short videos – *The Extraordinary Power of Forgiveness* and *How to Forgive* – which are available on YouTube. Whether or not you feel you have deep issues to face in this regard, they're a very good place to start with their straightforward and honest overview and practical advice. You can also find a transcript of both at the back of this book.

Even if you feel that you have no such issues to deal with, it's a timely reminder to review and, if necessary, revise how you live, how you operate in relationships and how you can ensure that you keep short accounts – ready and willing to forgive and ask for forgiveness.

It's not only about forgiveness, of course; as we saw in the last chapter, it's also about speaking and demonstrating our love for others. It's about being quick to praise, encourage, show appreciation, telling someone you love them just for being themselves. It's about unconditional love and expressing the things that so often we don't put into words because it's embarrassing. We might say, 'Well, you KNOW I love you'. Maybe, but be honest... there's something about being on the receiving end of affirming words that releases something positive inside of us, making us feel a foot taller and putting a spring in our step.

Sadly, for many of us, negative words are far more commonplace. 'Sticks and stones may break my bones, but words will never harm me' must be the most fatuous lie ever encapsulated in a common saying.

Thankfully the lie has been challenged in verses penned by several poets seeking to paint a more accurate picture, such as Barrie Wade. His poem 'Truth'[1] speaks eloquently of harsh words spoken which linger as 'ghosts that haunt' us and 'swords that pierce and stick inside' us, leaving scars on tender minds and hearts that are remembered long after physical bruises and cuts have healed.

Unfortunately, none of the responses I came across went on to talk about the positive effect of affirming words. However, the truth remains that, just as negative words can crush us, so positive ones can bring life. Both can affect the recipients for a lifetime, even changing the trajectory of their lives. And, by the way, don't limit this to thinking only about your family

---

1   Wade, B 1989, *Conkers: Poems*, Oxford University Press, USA.

relationships, but every aspect of your life and the people you interact with — friends, colleagues, those who serve and strangers on the street.

In the bible it says, *'Words kill, words give life; they're either poison or fruit — you choose'* (Proverbs 18:21, *The Message*). Now that is power! Is it safe in our hands?

A friend of mine recently lost a much-loved aunt and I was struck by the wonderful comment she made about her; that 'she loved well'. Wow! I would love to have such a thing said about me — more than anything else, I think. So how do we 'love well'? It's so easy to become swamped by life, to be so busy that we have to schedule times to 'just be' with one another, but simply (?!) changing how we live in relation to one another can bring transformation. Learning to praise and encourage one another as freely as we find fault and rebuke one another is a great place to start. Skip back to the last chapter and re-read the paragraphs about relationships and maybe take a few minutes to jot down anything that comes to mind before reading on.

Alongside these important and life-giving matters that affect our whole lives are the more practical issues to do with the end of life, but which should be dealt with now. We've already mentioned some of the reasons why we procrastinate when it comes to 'putting our affairs in order'. Probably the strongest one is that we believe we have plenty of time; wills, Lasting Powers of Attorney and such like are for old people, aren't they? Deep down, we know that is a very weak argument. We know that serious illness, accidents, or any other event you may want to name can affect us at any age. Yet, somehow, we humans have a remarkable ability to stick our heads in the sand and continue on our merry way, effectively gambling that it will all be okay in the end.

Does it really matter?
Absolutely!
Am I just scaremongering?
No!

There are some things which, if left undone, could create havoc for our nearest and dearest, not least our children. We're not only talking about what happens after death; we could also be exposing ourselves to the danger of our lives being administrated by the state instead of the people we know, love and trust. At the very least, leaving things undone can cause delays, expense, confusion and difficulty for those trying to stand in the gap. Maybe you consider yourself as someone who doesn't take unnecessary risks, but failing to put things in order and make your wishes clear is taking the biggest risk of all.

Whatever may come our way, our affairs need to be properly managed. We're talking here about the management of everything we own or are responsible for, namely assets (money, property, possessions and investments, etc.), potentially minor children or other dependants, or you may own a business. On death, of course, this becomes known as our 'estate'. Could we be leaving others to deal with our debts, or might our heirs lose out simply because we never got around to making the best arrangements possible to leave them well cared for?

Have you ever considered…

- What if I can no longer look after myself or my affairs?
- What will happen to my property and possessions when I die? Who gets what?
- What would happen to my children if anything happened to me?
- Do I have specific views and desires that need to be implemented?

It's important to realise that this isn't all about you; in fact, it's far less about you and much more about the people you love who will have to pick up the pieces or suffer the consequences. If something unexpected happens, it's so much better for them if you've had those difficult conversations, shared your thoughts and desires and, where necessary, ensured that things are in order, legally and practically. If you've ever had to deal with managing things when someone you love dies, you know how difficult it can be. It's tough enough to deal with practicalities when you're working through grief and loss, let alone having to do it all in the midst of chaos.

Some of the key issues to think about include:

- What about the children?
- Who do I want to inherit my money, property and possessions?

- What would happen if I could no longer manage my own life?
- Would I want to be resuscitated?
- Where are all my important documents and papers?

... and many more. The following chapters focus on the essential matters to be considered and acted upon and, as you do that, you will begin to identify the topics for these 'essential conversations'.

To think about

- What are the things that have come to mind as you've read this chapter? If necessary, go back over them and highlight them for yourself. What action do you need to take?
- How do you operate in relationships? How aware are you of causing or handling offence? How good are you at affirming people?
- What stood out for you in this chapter? What 'sore places' were touched? Were there some surprising memories or revelations?
- How do you need to change?
- Think about words that have greatly impacted you, good or bad. What can you learn from them to influence your behaviour, whether with close family/friends, colleagues and even casual encounters in daily life?
- How 'safe' are your words?
- What would you love to have said about you? Does that mean you need to change how you think, speak, or act?

NOTES FROM THIS CHAPTER

4 WHERE THERE'S A WILL ...

Getting to grips with essentials we'd rather ignore

> "There is something about wills which brings out the worst side of human nature. People who under ordinary circumstances are perfectly upright and amiable, go as curly as corkscrews and foam at the mouth, whenever they hear the words 'I devise and bequeath.'"
> —Dorothy L. Sayers, *Strong Poison*

Let's look now at these key areas; why do they need thought and action sooner rather than later and where do you start? Please note that while I have included quite a bit of information, it is by no means exhaustive, nor am I a legal professional, so please do your own research thoroughly and make sure you have the most up-to-date information, as legislation changes! I have given a few recommendations of reliable sources to get you started.

As the title suggests, let's start with wills and – a word to the wise – don't skip this chapter, even if you have a valid will. Take the time and opportunity to review your current situation and ensure that your existing will still covers everything as you would like.

A properly drawn up and executed (signed) will is a legally binding document and the only means by which you can control what happens to your assets when you die. A popular and incorrect assumption made by many is that a will isn't important, because if they die without having made one (i.e. they died 'intestate'), everything will automatically go to their spouse/partner, whether married, in a civil partnership or a long-term relationship. This assumption is definitely not correct in the UK where things even differ from nation to nation. Far from it; without a valid will, your estate (money, property and possessions) will be divided according to the 'rules of intestacy', which may be quite different to what you want to happen.

Hang on... 'rules of intestacy' – what are they?!

The UK government website has a helpful online questionnaire you can play with, which is fascinating. Just go to gov.uk and search 'intestacy' and you'll be taken to the page where you can find out the facts and access the questionnaire. You can put in several scenarios and, in most cases, there could be distant relatives who would inherit. I tried a more extreme scenario – that of a single person leaving no children, parents, brothers and sisters, half brothers and sisters, grandparents, aunts and uncles or half aunts and uncles, nephews and nieces, i.e. no living relatives... in which case their estate would simply go to the Crown! That's not referring to the Monarch, by the way!

Just as a taster, here are three case studies showing some facts as of December 2021.

SCENARIO ONE

- The deceased has a surviving partner (husband, wife or civil partner)
- The estate is likely to be worth more than a specific amount (set by government legislation)
- There are living children, grandchildren or other direct descendants (e.g. great-grandchildren)

England and Wales - if the estate is likely to be worth more than £270,000:

- The husband, wife or civil partner keeps all the assets (including property), up to £270,000, and all the personal possessions, whatever their value.
- The remainder of the estate will be shared as follows:
  - the husband, wife or civil partner gets an absolute interest in half of the remainder
  - the other half is then divided equally between the surviving children
  - If a son or daughter (or other child where the deceased had a parental role) has already died, their children will inherit in their place.

Scotland - if the estate is likely to be worth more than £473,000:

- The husband, wife or civil partner gets the house up to a value of £473,000. They'll get a lump sum of £473,000

if the house is worth more, and may have to sell off the property.
- They also get
    o furniture and moveable household goods up to the value of £29,000
    o up to £50,000 in cash
    o a third of the rest of the estate
- The children will get two-thirds of the rest of the estate.
    o If a son or daughter has already died, their children (the grandchildren of the deceased) will inherit in their place.

Northern Ireland - if the estate is likely to be worth more than £250,000:

- The husband, wife or civil partner keeps all the assets (including property), up to £250,000, and all the personal possessions, whatever their value.
- The husband, wife or civil partner must survive the deceased by at least 28 days to inherit.
- They also get one-third of the rest of the estate.
- The remaining two-thirds are shared between their children.
    o If a son or daughter has already died, their children (the grandchildren of the deceased) will inherit in their place.

- If the deceased had only one child, the following applies:
  - The husband, wife or civil partner keeps all the assets (including property), up to £250,000, and all the personal possessions, whatever their value.
  - The husband, wife or civil partner must survive the deceased by at least 28 days to inherit.
  - The remainder of the estate is divided in half between the
    - husband, wife or civil partner
    - son or daughter
    - If the son or daughter has already died, their children (the grandchildren of the deceased) will inherit in their parent's place.

SCENARIO TWO

- The deceased does not have a surviving partner (husband, wife or civil partner)
- There are living children, grandchildren or other direct descendants (e.g. great-grandchildren)

In this situation the same outcome applies across the UK as follows:

- The estate is shared equally between the children or their descendants.
- If a son or daughter has already died, their children (the grandchildren of the deceased) inherit in their place.

SCENARIO THREE

- The deceased does not have a surviving partner (husband, wife or civil partner).
- There are no living children, grandchildren or other direct descendants.
- There are surviving parents.

In England/Wales and Northern Ireland, the estate is shared equally between the parents. In Scotland, the estate is split in two, half going to the parents and half to the brothers or sisters. If a brother or sister has already died, their children (nieces and nephews of the deceased) inherit in their place.

Again, let me emphasise that what I'm setting out here applies to the UK and, if you live elsewhere, you must check the regulations in your country. However, it's also important to check that, wherever you live, you're using the latest information.

It's also vital to understand that in the UK if you are in a long-term relationship but not married or in a civil partnership, your partner has no automatic right to inherit and it may even mean that they can't continue to stay in the home you shared.

Do you still think it doesn't matter?! Hopefully not, so let's look at some of the issues to consider.

A will is a legally binding document, as long as it's been drawn up and signed correctly. While it takes time, thought, care and effort to draft, the reward is knowing that you've addressed several important issues, such as:

- Outlining how you want your estate (property, money, possessions) to be distributed, ensuring that it goes to the people (and perhaps causes) that matter to you most.
- Providing for your children – not just financially, but also appointing guardians to look after any who are aged under 18. Otherwise, the trauma of losing their parent may be made more traumatic by uncertainty and delays at a time when continuity and stability are key.
- Taking sensible action to protect assets for future generations. A will can address issues such as inheritance tax, and also make the best plans regarding property, business, investments, etc., ensuring that they are kept within the family and passed on as you desire.
- Outlining your preferences for your funeral and your wishes regarding burial or cremation. While of course it's not a jolly subject, it will certainly make life easier for your loved ones knowing that they're carrying out your wishes rather than guessing. It also means that potential arguments are stopped before they start!

A well-constructed and properly signed will can also help to avoid confusion and disputes. The last thing any of us wants is to have family disagreements flaring up. Getting everything set out clearly can prevent this and avoid adding stress to an already difficult time.

There are, of course, many websites offering advice, most being companies trying to sell their services and products. For straightforward information, I recommend the UK Government website (gov.uk) and that of Citizens Advice (citizensadvice.org.uk) both of which you can trust to be up to date. Just go to their home page and search 'making a will' and you should easily locate the information.

Having said that, let's look at some of the main things to consider.

Do you need to use a solicitor to draw up your will?

Not necessarily. However, as already mentioned, wills are legally binding documents and can be invalidated if not drafted, checked and signed in the correct manner. With this in view, unless your will is going to be straightforward and simple, it is wise to seek professional advice about it, as a mistake could prove costly after your death. A little time and investment now could save your estate significant sums in the long run and, most importantly, ensure as far as possible that your wishes are upheld.

There are three main routes to making a will from which you can choose. Before we look at them, we should note that, unlike many areas of financial services, will-writing is not a regulated market. This means that if something goes wrong, you may find yourself without protection or hope of compensation, depending on who wrote the will.

In this regard, using a solicitor gives you the most protection. While will-writing may not be regulated, solicitors ARE, which means that by using their services you are automatically covered by a range of potentially valuable protections.

This doesn't apply to other will-writing services (i.e. specialist companies who are not solicitors), meaning that you don't have the same potential protections. If you decide to write your own will, you are, of course, essentially on your own.

As the above illustrates, it matters who writes your will. However, protection isn't the only issue to take into account. Let's look at the three routes available:

Route one – Use a solicitor

Solicitors should know the law and write you a watertight will that does exactly what you want it to. Of course, there's no guarantee they will do a good job, but if something does go wrong you have more protection. Solicitors are regulated by the Solicitors Regulation Authority in England and Wales; Scotland and Northern Ireland have their own regulators. Wherever you may live, if problems arise, a complaint can be made to your solicitor's firm which, if not resolved, can be referred to the free Legal Ombudsman service for review.

A will drafted by a solicitor should give you the greatest peace of mind, especially if your affairs are complicated. A solicitor will be able to advise on the best will to address your situation and concerns, whether it's ensuring your partner is financially secure, protecting your children, your home, your business and other assets to name a few. Depending on your specific situation, it may be useful to set up a trust, which would definitely be better done by a professional. Whether it's a will or a trust, you want to ensure that your estate is divided as you wish. Some of the factors where it would be wise to get professional advice would include:

- A complex family situation, such as children with a former partner, or estranged children
- A vulnerable dependant whose interests you want to protect
- You own a business
- You have assets overseas
- Your estate may be liable to inheritance tax
- You wish to omit someone from your will who might, upon your death, then contest it

The main drawback of using a solicitor is, of course, the cost, as solicitors are generally the most expensive option. Costs for a simple will might start at around £200, while more complicated wills (for example, where you have been divorced, remarried and have children from your first marriage) can cost several hundred pounds. Specialist wills addressing some of the factors outlined above will likely start at £500. VAT will, of course, apply to all!

All is not lost, however! See the section below on 'Free wills'.

Route two – Use will-writing services

Will-writing services can be a low-cost alternative to using a solicitor, with prices sometimes starting at under £100. They're most suitable for people with straightforward circumstances, such as everything being left to immediate family members and no complications involved, such as overseas properties/investments, a business, etc.

While some companies have specialist staff checking the wills they produce, their staff may not have any legal qualifications and protections may be limited compared with using a regulated firm of solicitors, as outlined earlier. If you feel this may be the route for you, please check whether the company is a member of a recognised professional or trade body, such as the Institute of Professional Will-writers (ipw.org.uk/) or the Society of Will Writers (willwriters.com/). These bodies have codes of practice/conduct which members have agreed to follow and you can take complaints to them about member firms. IPW and SWW members also have professional indemnity insurance, which can provide compensation if something goes wrong.

However, while affording a degree of comfort, these organisations are voluntary and not official regulators. As such, enforcing rules and getting redress could be more difficult than with a Solicitors Regulation Authority-regulated solicitor, where you also have access to the Legal Ombudsman.

It's important to note that if you get your will drawn up by a solicitor or a will-writing service you are not obliged to appoint them as executors of your estate. Some people choose banks or solicitors, but fees can be very high, which depletes the value of your estate and the final value passed on to your beneficiaries. Make sure, then, that you only agree to this if it is what you want; it might be better to choose trusted friends or relatives.

Route three – Do it yourself

If your circumstances are very simple and straightforward, you can write your own will using one of the templates easily available online or from stationery shops. This is, of course, the cheapest option, so why might it not be a good idea? Mainly, if you make any mistakes, you won't have the protection you'd have if a solicitor had drawn up your will, as outlined earlier.

Suffice to say here that if you use a template, the company supplying it won't take responsibility for anything that may go wrong. So, while this route can be a cheap option, you are taking a risk that, if something does go wrong, there would be no recourse to compensation.

Again, do refer to the government's website regarding making a will.

Free or low-cost wills

In the UK, many charities offer access to free or low-cost will-drafting services. While this is in the hope of a bequest to the charity (a donation in your will), this isn't obligatory. If you do agree to leave a bequest to the charity, it will come out of your estate and is inheritance-tax deductible.

If you're 55 and over, you may be able to take advantage of Free Wills Month, which happens in March and October each year. Visit freewillsmonth.org.uk/ for details.

Please note that these free will-drafting services are for simple wills and are unlikely to apply if your situation is more complex. Also note that, while wills drafted under the Free Wills Month scheme are done by solicitors, some of those offered by charities are undertaken by will-writing companies, as covered above.

What information is useful when making a will?

Your will should cover your whole estate, so a good place to start is to draw up a list of all your assets and liabilities. If you use a professional service, they may start the process with a comprehensive questionnaire for you to complete.

Areas to cover include:

A. Personal details – everything about you, your family status, any former partnerships, children of your existing or former relationships, tax domicile, occupation, dependents, etc.

B. Executors

C. Funeral wishes (more on this in Chapter Six)

D. Provision for the care of minor children (more on this in Chapter Five)

E. Legacies (specific gifts of money or personal belongings) – draw up a list of the items and the full name of the person or cause (e.g. a favourite charity) you want the item to go to. Other items which may need to be allocated include:
   - Personal possessions (jewellery, furniture, furnishings, art, books, car, animals, musical instruments, clothing, wine, etc.)
   - Business assets, specifically, shares in your business
   - Property, including agricultural property

F. Residue – what you want to happen to what is left after all debts, tax, expenses/administration costs and legacies have been dealt with.

G. Financial details – everything (including deeds, mortgage details, etc.) relating to your main residence; details of other properties (both the UK and abroad) and what they are (holiday home, etc.); cash, bank accounts, investments, any personal possessions of significant value, policies, pensions, benefits (death in service, etc.), trusts, loans, details of regular payments and any sizeable debts, other than a mortgage.

Choosing an executor

It is key that you choose people you trust to act as your executors, who will ensure that your wishes are carried out fully and efficiently. Administrating someone's estate can entail a lot of work (depending on the complexity), so it's important to choose people who are competent and will deal with things in a good and timely manner.

Executors are responsible for collecting the assets of your estate, paying any debts and inheritance tax and, once all that has been done, distributing the estate to your beneficiaries. You can appoint between one to four executors, who must be aged 18 or over. If you appoint one or two, it may be wise to include a substitute executor in case one is unable or unwilling to act. The important thing is to choose people you trust and who you feel confident have the ability to handle your affairs in a good and timely manner. You should talk this through with those you would like to appoint, to make sure that they understand what is involved and are happy to act on your behalf.

Types of wills

While many of us would say that our lives are straightforward and simple, many have now become more complex than we may realise. As outlined earlier, at different times of life we find ourselves in changed circumstances. Some of the decisions and actions we have taken may have changed the landscape permanently.

Whichever season of life you're in, it's worth considering how you might safeguard and preserve your assets for your family and future generations. Take time to identify your circumstances, how you would like things to play out and what may be the stumbling blocks. You can then use these conclusions to see whether you can write your own will, or whether it would be wise to use a solicitor. It will also enable you to clearly present your circumstances and intentions to a solicitor to ensure that they give you the best advice and service.

It's definitely worth taking the time to research what is available. Some solicitors offer a variety of wills to cover different situations and seasons of life. This could include owning property overseas, a business, having children from previous relationships or with special needs, or wanting to protect your main residence from being sold to meet care home costs. You may well decide that using their services is money well spent to ensure that you achieve the best result.

Signing a will

For your will to be legally valid, it must be in writing and signed by you (the 'testator') in the presence of two independent witnesses. All three (you and both witnesses) must be present at the same time and see each other sign the will.

Anyone can be a witness to the signing of your will, as long as they are over the age of 18 and as independent as possible. *Please note* – a witness should *never* be someone who is named in your will as a beneficiary, or their close relative (e.g. spouse/partner). This would mean that, while the will would still be valid, they would not be able to inherit under it (Section 15 Wills Act 1837).

Storing your will

While it may seem to be stating the obvious, let's just note that your will should be stored safely and that you ensure that your executors know where that is, so that they can easily find it after your death. You can, of course, keep it at home, obviously taking care to ensure that it is stored as securely as possible to avoid loss or damage.

Your solicitor, should you choose that route to write your will, will store the original document for you, generally free of charge, providing you with a scanned copy of the signed (engrossed) document for your records.

Some will-writing services will also store your will, but there may be a charge for this. There is also a potential risk here, as I discovered when the company that wrote my original will ceased trading. Sadly, they failed to notify their clients of this and alas, my will was never seen again!

If you live in England and Wales, you can store your will with HM Courts and Tribunals Service (formerly the Probate Office). Currently there's a £20 fee for this service, but withdrawing it is free. Again, information is available on both the UK Government and Citizens Advice websites. Other possibilities for storing your will may include your bank, although that could become problematic depending on their terms and conditions, so do carefully check that out before making decisions. They will also charge for the service.

It's important to note that the *original* will is required when probate is applied for. While it is possible to make an application to the Probate Registry to admit a *copy* of a will, it's a complex and time-consuming process and could lead to all manner of complications. The moral here? Ensure the safe storage of your original will and that its whereabouts are known to your executors. Keeping a copy of your signed will amongst your important papers is important for your own records and could, if the original document is lost, save the day. However, it's a poor second choice and unnecessary if you make good arrangements in the first place.

Reviewing your will

Time does not stand still! Your personal circumstances change as life continues and it is recommended that you review your will every five years and/or after any major change in your life. The UK Government website suggests that such changes may include:

- Getting married or entering into a civil partnership – upon either event, if you live in England, Wales or Northern Ireland, your will is automatically revoked

- Getting separated or divorced – this does not automatically invalidate a will made during the marriage, so failing to make changes could lead to results far from your current wishes
- Having a child (or you may want to provide for 'new' grandchildren)
- Moving house
- If an executor named in your will dies

Don't forget that rules differ in the UK from nation to nation, so do make sure that you clarify the situation where you live.

Personal items

As well as the major issues to be planned and provided for in your will, there may be other items that you want to go to specific people, such as jewellery, art, family heirlooms, family history documents, etc.

This is something well worth thinking through. It may be important to spell out some of these items in your will, but think too about those which may have more sentimental than financial value and which could only too easily be taken by the 'wrong' person! It can be these actions that cause offence and division in a family because someone simply decided that they wanted something 'unspecified'. You know how it can be. You've always loved a certain item in your grandmother's home, but nothing was said and, after her death, someone else swooped in and took it before you could even say anything!

You may also have items that are special to you simply because of what they represent, items that could be easily overlooked. I have a number of these around and have told my executors that I am going to leave an inventory with photos of certain items, simply so that they know what they may be throwing away! Let's face it, when I'm no longer around I won't care, but I do want at least to ensure that my family knows what they're taking to a charity shop or, even worse, to the local recycling centre. It doesn't take long to take a photo and add a brief caption so that they *know* that this crystal vase was one of their great-grandparents' wedding presents, or that those little leather cases were hand-made by their 'portmanteau-maker' great grandfather for their grandmother when she was a small child – and so on.

It's not always about the monetary value; some items represent a wonderfully tangible link to previous generations of our family and weave a thread of continuity into the fabric of who we are. I realised how precious this could be after my sister died and, in the final sorting out of the family home, I came across a folder of her paintings, three of which are now on my wall. Was she a famous artist? No, but she most certainly was a beloved daughter/sister/wife/mother/grandmother/aunt and great aunt and it's such a joy to look at them and remember…

There are items which I fully intend to pass on to some in our younger generation before I die, explaining what they are, who they belonged to and why they're precious, entrusting these tangible links to be appreciated, valued and stewarded for future generations. Not a bad thing to do in this instant and throw-away generation, I think!

So that's the first step, but by no means the last! Read on for further important issues to think through, starting with provision for minor children and possible action to take. But, before you move on...

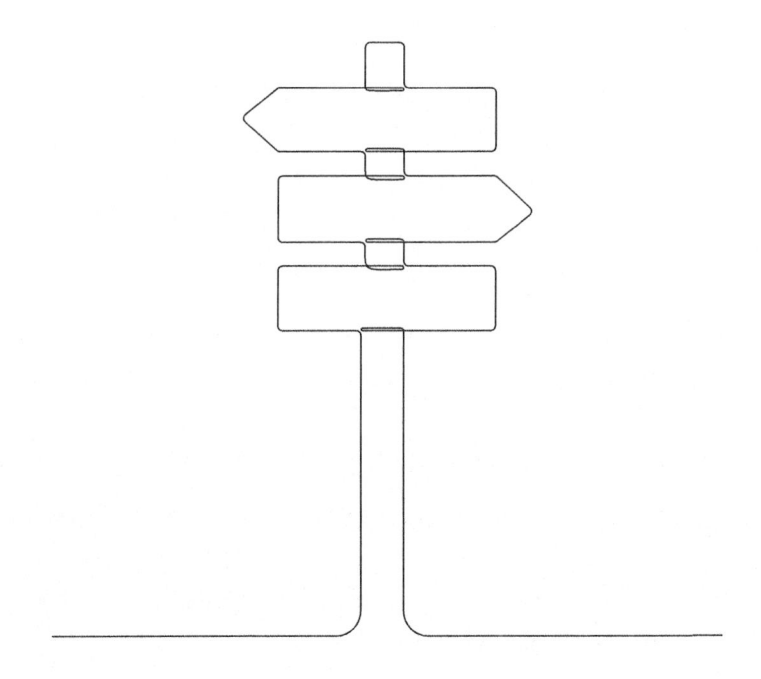

To think about

If you already have a will, get it out (assuming you know where it is!) and go through it again in the light of this chapter.

- Is it still relevant to your circumstances?
- Do any of the categories mentioned apply to you? For instance, you now have children; you've started a business; you're looking ahead to the inevitability of requiring additional care; you're planning to marry in the coming year.
- Will it matter if you take no action? Be honest about this; don't just take the line of least resistance!
- Do your executors know where your original will is stored?

If you haven't yet made a will:

- Why? Are your reasons still valid in light of what you've just read, or do you need to act?
- Create your plan of action and work through it.

Special items:

- Are there items special to you that you need to earmark specifically or give away now?
- What are they?
- Who should they go to?
- How can you make sure they understand the significance of what you're giving to them?

NOTES FROM THIS CHAPTER

5 THE YOUNG ONES...

Caring for your greatest treasure

> "My children are gifts, they remind me of what's important."
> —Elle Macpherson

For a parent, undoubtedly the most sensitive issue that you never want to think about is what would happen to your children if you were to die while they were under 18. Such a horrifying thought gives us a huge dilemma and, all too often, the issue becomes another casualty of procrastination and denial. Thinking about such a scenario and how to make the best decisions for our children is so daunting that we simply don't go there, but to what potential conclusion?

No one knows exactly how many children under the age of 18 lose a parent each year, let alone both parents. However, in the UK it is estimated that, on average, a child under the age of 16 is bereaved of a parent every 22 minutes of each day (Winston's Wish – winstonswish.org/about-us/facts-and-figures/).

People often assume that making a will is just about property and inheritance. Crucially, it is also about making provision for your children, possibly the most important plan you could ever make. Your will, as a legal document, ensures that your children receive what you want them to have in the event of your death. Dying without having made a will may, as we have already noted, cost those now managing our affairs unnecessary time, effort and expense. In the case of minor children, it may also add unnecessary distress and uncertainty at the very time they desperately need to feel secure, safe and comforted.

Parents who have parental responsibility (more on this below) can appoint a legal guardian to care for their children if they die while the child is under 18. The requirements for such an appointment are similar to the requirements of putting a will in place, i.e. it needs to be in writing and signed in the presence of two witnesses. This is why it makes sense for the appointment of guardians to be incorporated within the terms of your will.

Probably, the most common reason for avoiding this important question is simply the difficulty of choosing the right person/people to take on this role. The very thought of someone replacing us and raising our children shakes our foundations, stirring up so many emotions that it can be hard to think straight, and so we bury the issue. There are so many things to think about: will those you are considering be able to manage physically, or are they approaching an age where caring for young children may be too much for them? Are you thinking of family members, or would a close family friend be the best choice? If you have more than one child, who could accommodate both/all together? Do they share your general outlook on life? Faith? What about the finances? And on it goes.

Another reason for procrastination may be the mistaken assumption that your children would automatically go to family. That may well be the outcome, but in the UK, if both parents die without having appointed a guardian for their minor children, those bereaved children become the responsibility of the court and, until the court appoints a guardian, the children might be taken into care; surely something you would want to avoid at all costs.

Family life can be complicated! These days, it's not particularly unusual to find children whose parents aren't married, or who have divorced. What many don't realise is that guardian appointments can only take effect if there is no one else alive who already has parental responsibility and normally, the terms of such an appointment would state that it only takes effect if both parents have died.

Let's quickly clarify parental responsibility. Basically, if the biological mother and father are married when a child is born, they will both have parental responsibility. However, if they were unmarried at the time, only the mother will automatically have parental responsibility. The father can acquire parental responsibility if:

- he marries the mother
- he becomes registered as the child's father

- he and the mother make a 'Parental Responsibility Agreement'
- the court, on his application, orders that he shall have parental responsibility for the child

For information about parental responsibility, visit the UK Gov website (gov.uk) and search for 'parental responsibility'.

So, dear reader, if you're a parent of minor children, please, please, please don't delay further. Yes, it's a tough one, but you know it makes sense! You can appoint more than one guardian and/or a substitute guardian or guardians. Parents can appoint different guardians, but, for obvious reasons, they should ideally consult each other and appoint the same person or persons.

There's a lot to think about. To make sure that you make the best decisions and provisions for your children, it would almost certainly be wise to consult a solicitor to ensure that you cover all the bases, particularly if your family situation is complex in any way. I would heartily recommend that you include this when you make your will. If you've already made a will that covers everything else and you don't want to change it, then you can either make a codicil to that will or draw up a specific document to put in place the appointment of guardians.

Where to start?

The starting point is to begin to think through who, other than you, would be the best choice, able to step into the breach and provide a stable and caring home for your children. You will, of course, want to consider your options carefully, so here are some things to throw into the pot to help your discussions.

The first choice is often likely to be other family members and maybe your own parents could be an option. However, here are a few things to ponder:

- Think about your own childhood – do you want the same for your children?
- What's the relationship like between your child and their grandparents?
- How old are your parents and your child/children? Will they be able to cope physically?

Another strong possibility is to appoint guardians from your wider family. But, how do you choose if there are many?

Whether you're looking at family members or friends, here are some further thoughts and questions:

- Would the person you're thinking of want the responsibility?
- Do they already have children? Do you have a similar parenting style and similar values to those of the person you want to nominate?
- What about religious or ethical beliefs?
- What about the geographical locations? Does the proposed guardian live locally, or in another part of the country? Would your child have the upheaval of relocating, making new friends, starting a new school, etc.?

- If you have more than one child, who would be the best option so they can stay together?
- If you have an only child, would they be overwhelmed at being part of a family with 'siblings'?
- Would your chosen person have enough time, energy and financial capacity to care for your child until adulthood?
- Will your child/children be happy with your decision?

Picking up on the last point, what about your children's views? Obviously, you wouldn't sit them down and say that you'd like to know who they would like to live with if you die – that hopefully goes without saying! However, you might be able to get a feel of how they feel around different people, which you can then take into account when making your final decision.

Once you've settled on your choice of guardian(s) you will, of course, need to discuss this with them before proceeding to name them in your will. You also need to think through issues around your property, finances, etc. and whether you want these affairs managed by the guardian(s), or whether it would be best to appoint someone else to handle this. You may be moving into the area of setting up a trust, in which case you would be best served to seek professional advice to make sure that whatever is put in place is the best possible solution.

And please – if you decide to appoint two separate individuals to manage your will and the care of your children, make sure that they are in good relationship!

One other curve ball to flag – your chosen guardians are permitted to appoint replacement guardians for your children, in their own wills, which you would probably want to take into consideration and discuss with them. As advised earlier regarding your will, it's wise to review your decisions over time as circumstances may change – both yours and those of the prospective guardian.

As with all the matters we're thinking about in this chapter, it is important that your family members know of the arrangements you have made for your children, so that any transition can be made carefully and swiftly to ensure as much ease as possible for them.

These things aren't easy, but no one ever said that being a parent was a piece of cake! What is true is that taking courage and addressing these important, tough questions will give you a peace of mind that you didn't realise was missing!

To think about

- Do you need to commit to take action rather than procrastinate? How will you do that?
- What is your legal position? Who has parental responsibility for your children? Do you need professional advice to ensure you understand your situation?
- Who do you need to talk to – especially a former spouse?
- Use this chapter as a guide for working through the different issues; make a note of everything that applies to your situation and then work out your plan of action.

MARJIE SUTTON

NOTES FROM THIS CHAPTER

6 STAYING AHEAD OF THE GAME

Prevention rather than cure

"Planning is bringing the future into the present so that you can do something about it now."

—Alan Lakein

Getting a good and sound will in place is an excellent start, but only deals with ensuring that your wishes are carried out after your death. What about during your lifetime? Don't sit back and relax too soon! There's more to think about and act upon before you can tick all the boxes.

LASTING POWER OF ATTORNEY (LPA)

What on earth are LPAs and why do they matter? In a nutshell, they enable you to decide, while you can, who you would like to be managing your affairs should you find yourself unable to do so. Don't switch off here if you're under 50; these aren't matters purely for people in their dotage or with special needs. We all know that our lives can change in an instant, sometimes leaving us dependent upon other people to help us make crucial choices about our future.

Most of us somehow manage to park that thought and proceed merrily along, comforting ourselves that we can worry about that when it happens. But stop and think. What if the unexpected does happen? You may be assuming that your family can just step in and take care of everything, but the government's website tells a different story.

'If you lose mental capacity, through illness or injury, and haven't created an LPA:

- *you'll no longer be able to decide who makes decisions for you (you can only make your LPA while you still have mental capacity)*
- *people you don't know could end up making crucial decisions for you instead – such as whether to accept medical treatment to keep you alive, or about what you eat and wear, and where you live*
- *your family or friends might have to go to court to make decisions on your behalf – which can be a lot more expensive and time-consuming than making an LPA.'*

Should you find yourself in such a situation, someone may need to apply to the Court of Protection to become your deputy, which gives them similar powers to those of an attorney. A relative or friend can apply to be your deputy; alternatively, a professional may be appointed. So, all is not lost, but, as the above quote notes, the process of becoming a deputy is a lot more time-consuming and expensive than setting up an LPA. A deputy must also do some things on an ongoing basis, such as paying an annual fee and submitting an annual report, so it is usually easier for someone to be an attorney rather than a deputy.

I don't know about you, but I'd rather my affairs were managed by those I love and trust rather than strangers, so I've taken my own advice and set up LPAs. It's a remarkably straightforward process.

There are two LPAs available; one covering property and finances and the other health and welfare. It's wise to set up both. These matters come under the care of the Office of the Public Guardian and are fully explained in the guide found on the government's website (gov.uk – search 'lasting powers of attorney').

Don't be overwhelmed; it's an easy process to follow. It takes time to think through some of the issues and talk to those you want to be your attorneys but doing that is, in itself, a really good exercise as we think through some of the tough questions referred to earlier – the 'what if' questions. They need a response – 'if ... then this is what I want to happen'.

You can do the whole job yourself, either online or by downloading paper versions of the forms on the government website. You need to take care and follow the instructions in detail, but they are clear and without jargon. At the time of writing, the cost for registering each LPA is £82.

You can, of course, get a solicitor to do this on your behalf, but it will cost appreciably more than doing it yourself, on average around £500+VAT for a single person applying for both types, plus the two £82 registration fees. It's a bit of a no-brainer unless you have a particularly complex set of circumstances to navigate. The guides on the gov.uk website mentioned above set things out very clearly and can help you to decide how you want to proceed.

While this is a straightforward process, it isn't a fast one. Once you have completed everything, you will need to send the signed documents to the Office of the Public Guardian for registration, which may take several weeks. It's worth paying the extra postage to send these using guaranteed next-day delivery. If all is in order, you will receive sealed copies confirming registration and a link to enable you to set up your own account. Should your attorneys need to begin acting on your behalf, they will need to know how to access this. A helpful guide to their duties is also available for attorneys on the government website.

Making a health and welfare LPA has the helpful effect of causing you to at least stop and think about possible scenarios (hopefully a long way ahead) that could mean decisions being made on your behalf about issues that you actually have strong views on, such as life-sustaining treatment. Depending on how strongly you feel, you may find it helpful to clarify your thoughts, which may be done by making:

ADVANCE DECISIONS AND STATEMENTS

The NHS provides very clear and helpful guidance about this; to quote their definitions in a nutshell:

*An **advance decision** (sometimes known as an advance decision to refuse treatment, an ADRT, or a living will) is a decision you can make now to refuse a specific type of treatment at some time in the future. It lets your family, carers and health professionals know your wishes about refusing treatment if you're unable to make or communicate those decisions yourself.*

*An **advance statement** is a written statement that sets down your preferences, wishes, beliefs and values regarding your future care. The aim is to provide a guide to anyone who might have to make decisions in your best interest if you have lost the ability to make or communicate decisions.*

More detailed information and guidance about both can be found on the NHS website, nhs.uk. Search 'advance statement'.

Whether you decide to pursue one of these routes or not, it's a worthwhile exercise to do the thinking and then discuss it with your attorneys and/or family members so that they are aware of your thoughts and wishes. You may want to spell it out or, like me, after a healthy conversation with my attorneys, conclude together that there is total trust between us and we're all happy to leave decisions with them. It gives you the opportunity to make a choice, rather than sudden events taking that possibility away. It also ensures that your attorneys are comfortable with potentially making such decisions.

While we're thinking about these somewhat daunting issues, let's think too about:

ORGAN DONATION

Obviously, this question will only arise as an end-of-life decision, but in the flow of thinking about the matters just discussed, it seems good to add this in here. Organ donation is something that often stirs strong responses, both for and against. Some people feel passionately that they want their organs used upon their death; some, for varied reasons, feel just as strongly that they don't; while others simply haven't thought about it. There is also a lot of misunderstanding about the whole subject. The NHS has an excellent dedicated website – organdonation.nhs.uk/ - which sets out the facts and answers all your questions, providing everything you need to know in order to make an informed decision.

Again, it's crucial that you communicate your wishes to those who need to know, particularly your executors, close family and attorney(s). If you've made a health and welfare LPA, you will, of course, have discussed this with your attorney(s) when you set this up.

CARE IN LATER LIFE

For many, one of the hardest things to think about is what happens to us if we reach a time when we simply cannot continue to care for ourselves. For most people, the thought of losing our independence and being dependent on others is a bitter pill to swallow. Even if we can live with family members, the worry of 'being a burden' can weigh heavily. Let's be honest, for most of us, the subject is daunting and not a little depressing. Perhaps this isn't yet your dilemma and this prospect is many years away from you, but you may instead find yourself in the position of seeking to support an older relative and, again, it can feel like a minefield.

However, many people have found solutions that work really well for them, whether it's getting the support necessary to stay in their home or some other solution There are many alternatives to consider and, while we all hope never to have to 'go there', it's not a bad thing to at least wise up so that we're armed with information. The NHS website has helpful guides on end-of-life care, as does *Which?* (which.co.uk), with excellent articles and guides covering virtually everything you need to think about. Search 'how to choose the right care in later life' to access these. If you reach a point where this moves from information gathering to actually making plans, your GP will be a good place to start with their knowledge both of patient and resources.

It's really important to talk about these things too. If you're making a health and welfare LPA, that's an ideal time to chat things through with your attorney(s) and, of course, with any other close family members. What is key is to have honest and open conversations so that, together, you've reached conclusions that you're all happy with.

END-OF-LIFE WISHES – FUNERALS

It amused me to realise that 'funeral' is an anagram for 'real fun'! That said, planning your own funeral may sound creepy and surely joins the list of topics none of us wants to think about right now! However, you may know from experience that it's often difficult for relatives to make arrangements while they're grieving, let alone possibly having to navigate different and strong opinions. So, once again, doing some forward thinking and communicating your wishes helps to avoid unnecessary stress or worries about whether they've 'done right' by you and hopefully, in some cases, keep feathers smooth and unruffled.

While you can include your wishes regarding your funeral in your will, these directions are not legally binding and, in any event, it's possible that your will won't be read until after the funeral. With that in mind, it's clearly sensible to make a point of letting your executors and/or close family know your wishes about this, and also organ donation if that's important to you.

What do you need to think about? Here are some starter questions:

- Do you have any specific wishes regarding your funeral?
- What would you like to be done regarding a gathering?
- What form would you like that to take and do you have any preferences about music, who to speak, flowers, etc?
- Do you want your body to be buried or cremated? Do you have any specific requests regarding a burial plot, or what to do with the ashes?

Many people now are looking at more 'green' possibilities and simple funerals, or even DIY possibilities. Whether you want to pursue this or go the more traditional route of engaging a funeral director, there is, inevitably, a huge amount of information to be found on the internet, from the straightforward and factual, to the weird and wacky! I always prefer to start with independent advice, which can be found from Citizens Advice, *Which?* (both mentioned earlier) and Natural Death (http://naturaldeath.org.uk/). AgeUK also has a very helpful factsheet which can be downloaded directly from their website (ageuk.org.uk/).

The price of funerals is often a huge shock to families and it is worth looking into pre-paid funeral plans and insurance. Again, there are many options available, but the following websites are good places to start, as they provide up-to-date information and advice without an agenda to sell a specific product:

Which? -
which.co.uk

Money Helper -
moneyhelper.org.uk
Money Saving Expert -
moneysavingexpert.com

Since July 2022, providers of pre-paid funeral plans have been required to be regulated by the Financial Conduct Authority. This has been introduced as a measure to 'enhance' consumer protection and introduce high standards so that plans are sold fairly, perform as expected and provide value for money. If you decide to buy a pre-paid plan, do make sure that the provider is duly regulated.

An alternative to buying a funeral plan could be to put money aside in a designated account, which your executor can access. Whichever route you choose, it would be both kind and thoughtful to have thought this through. This will ensure that your executor and/or family aren't faced with having to meet considerable costs before your estate is finalised and funds released, or, even worse, to cover the costs themselves because you haven't made provision.

The funeral industry as such is unregulated, so there is no standard code of practice or complaints procedure, although many funeral directors belong to one of the professional organisations listed below. These organisations require their members to follow strict codes of conduct, complaints procedures and price transparency policies and offer an independent arbitration scheme in the case of disputes.

National Association for Funeral Directors (NAFD) – nafd.org.uk

National Society of Allied and Independent Funeral Directors (SAIF) saif.org.uk

Is that it?!

Probably, but possibly not! We've already touched on special items, some of sentimental value rather than financial. As a wonderfully unique individual, there may be other things in your life that are deeply important to you. For example, maybe you have a much-loved pet, so take the time to think about it and what might happen if you were no longer around. Where would it go, and who would look after it?

Of course, none of the above is an easy task, but they're very worthwhile. Perhaps the thought of the potential cost involved is causing you to hold back, but dealing with these matters surely has to rate as important as holidays, outings and other such like and deserves as much consideration. Getting professional help will cost and may not always be necessary, but it *is* important to talk to people who know their stuff. Personal recommendations are good, so ask around your family and friends for any.

Finally (for this chapter anyway!), a word to the wise. Do make sure that you keep your information up to date, for example, if you move house, get married, divorced or... Sometimes, it's a question of simply ensuring that your correct details are recorded, but it could make a material difference, such as a will becoming invalid upon marriage.

While it may seem a huge and overwhelming task, once it's done you can relax, knowing that you've done all you can to make the way as simple and smooth as possible and that things are done just as you would like.

To think about

- What boxes can you tick as completed? Do they still reflect your wishes? Are the details still up to date?
- Use the chapter to work through the different issues, even if some of them seem remote for you at this stage of life. Which do you need to seriously think about and act on now? When will you return to the others?
- Are there conversations you need to have with family/friends about your thoughts and wishes? Or about theirs?

NOTES FROM THIS CHAPTER

MARJIE SUTTON

7 LIVING LIGHTLY

Clearing the decks to make space for life

> "We must be willing to let go of the life we have planned, so as to have the life that is waiting for us."
> —E M Forster

If you've just ploughed through the 'essentials', you may be feeling overwhelmed and ready to put the book back on the shelf! However, having come this far, let's not become 'weary in well doing', but keep pushing through. In addition to having all the legal matters (will, LPAs, etc.) in place, there are other things you can do to streamline. While not essential in the same way as the legal matters are, the benefits are real, both for you and especially for those acting on your behalf.

At some point in the future, your executors will have to go through all your affairs in order to carry out your wishes regarding everything you've accumulated. Two things in particular will be an enormous help to them and can also bring you benefit here and now, namely a record of everything about you – let's call it your 'life data bank' (more below) – and a comprehensive schedule of all your assets and liabilities.

This exercise may prove to be something of a surprise. Most people would say that their lives were pretty simple, but when you start gathering all the information together, it can be quite a shock to see the amount of detail that forms and shapes us. What a good opportunity to review, revise, and perhaps cull some of the clutter and, once it's done, you can sleep easy, knowing that you have everything at your fingertips. More importantly, your executors or attorneys will have as simple a task as possible. It can actually be amazingly therapeutic to get on top of things and suddenly realise that the 'weight' that's been lurking in your subconscious mind has gone.

Let's start with assets and liabilities. In a nutshell, this means anything you own which has a positive monetary value (assets) and any financial obligations, loans, debts which must be paid (liabilities). For example:

Assets might include any/all of the following, with current market (resale) value:

- Cash/money in the bank
- Property – both your main home and any second homes, caravans, boats, etc.
- Vehicles
- Investments such as ISAs, stocks/shares, bonds, etc.
- Other financials, e.g. pensions, life insurance, death in service benefits etc.

- Other valuable personal items, e.g., jewellery, art, musical instruments, photographic equipment, computers, etc. – in particular (but not exclusively), any items for which you have special insurance in place
- Loans you may have made to someone that are still outstanding

Liabilities would include:

- Mortgage(s)
- Personal loans
- Car loans etc.
- Credit card outstanding balances
- Student loans
- Direct debits etc.

All of this information can be kept in your life data bank, but it would be helpful to also have it in a stand-alone schedule for easy reference. Your executors will definitely need this in order to manage your estate and it will also help you to keep track of your own affairs.

Life data bank

So, what is this 'life data bank'? Call it what you like, in simple terms it's a record of everything that makes your life work. It's surprising, when you begin to catalogue all the details of your life, to realise just how many there are! From important documents to details of things such as bank accounts, investments, health data, household affairs... let alone numerous passwords! It's bad enough keeping track ourselves, so imagine for a moment what a nightmare sorting out your affairs could be for your executors. How will they fare? Will it be a walk in the park, or like being parachuted into a strange place with no map and, possibly, not understanding the language?

Depending on your creativity, or maybe your competence with technology, there are several ways in which you can record all your vital information. The key thing is that information should be clear, up to date, easy for executors/attorneys to access, yet secure. If you're happy with using the computer, possibly the most straightforward solution is a spreadsheet, with different categories of information stored on separate tabs. You may prefer a Word document or similar, or even pen and paper. Whatever route you choose, the most important things to remember are to keep it updated, in a safe place and its location made known to your attorneys/executors. It's probably good not to go for too many bells and whistles, but to keep it simple!

So, what might you need to include? I've come up with nine categories that should be considered, plus ideas of what might be included under each heading:

1. Personal data: Everything about you, family/dependents, wider family, key contacts

2. Property: Where you live: If you own your home, where are the deeds kept? If you rent, include details of tenancy – landlord, tenancy agreement, etc. Include second homes, caravans, etc.

3. Health: Providers – doctor, dentist, optician, etc.; specific details such as vaccinations, health apps, activities such as gym memberships or slimming clubs

4. Lifestyle: Memberships; household details – utilities, traders, insurance, TV/phone/broadband; subscriptions; local authority; motoring organisations, etc.

5. Financials: Bank accounts; cards; insurances; card protection; investments; professional adviser details (accountant, financial advisor); savings; pensions; assets and liabilities; tax affairs

6. Legals: Attorneys; executors; solicitor; documents

7. Work: If you run your own business – details, partners, employees, clients/suppliers, website/social media. If you're an employee – details of employer. Domains, email accounts, virus protection, backups, professional body memberships

8. Security: Passwords; logins; PINs; important documents – what and where are they? For example, birth/marriage certificates, divorce papers, will, LPAs, contracts, investments, e.g. share certificates, passport, driving license, car documents, household documents – tenancy agreement, insurances, etc.

9. End of life: Executors, location of will, funeral plan, life insurance, burial/cremation/ashes, advance decisions/ statements, organ donation, people to notify – friends/

contacts; providers (e.g. landlord), funeral service/wake, special gifts, family memorabilia, etc.

I can't emphasise enough the importance of regularly updating this information, such as changes of address, new bank/credit cards, change of suppliers and so on. If you can get into the habit of doing this on a regular basis, you'll keep it easy to handle. For many of us, that's a challenge because it's tedious; we'd rather be doing something 'nice'. It's all too easy to think, 'I'll do that later', but then we forget and ultimately find ourselves with information that's totally out of date, or faced with a task of updating that is now a huge chore instead of a two-minute job.

One thing that works for me is a monthly slot where I deal with household finances and accounts. I have a simple spreadsheet setting out all my monthly payments with due dates, so it's an easy task to set up payments and ensure that my bank account will be in funds at the right time. It never takes long, and it's easy to add five minutes on to that session to update my life data bank. Sorted, over a cup of coffee (and/or sneaky chocolate biscuit!).

Another wise habit to build into your life rhythm is an annual review of where you're at and what may have changed or is about to, and whether that requires changes to your will, etc. Again, this is something that often lands up on the 'to-do' list, which is fine, unless your list could be more correctly entitled '*should* do but...'!

And so much more...

Having talked about bringing order to everything that could be said to form the structure of our lives, let's switch gears to another aspect of living lightly, namely taking stock of your life and what it contains, with a view to being more streamlined. In the West, we live in a culture of 'stuff', often the more the merrier. Sadly for some, their possessions affirm their success, or somehow shape their identity. How interesting, then, that one of the main benefits of the Covid-19 emergency in the UK was people taking the opportunity of being 'locked down' at home to go through their possessions and have a good old clear out! So much so, that charity shops couldn't cope with the sudden and continuous avalanche of goods!

Being a minimalist has become very fashionable in some quarters and it's interesting to observe the different ways people respond to the trend. Some can be quite ruthless in disposing of items no longer needed, some suffer from the 'it might come in useful' syndrome and can convince themselves of all sorts of reasons why nothing should change. For others, the thought of getting rid of clothes and other items takes them to the edge of trauma! Well, perhaps I'm exaggerating here, but come on, have a long and honest look at yourself and everything cluttering up (oops! Of course, I should have said 'enhancing') your home!

It's time to be radical, disciplined and uncluttered, with the added bonus of being able to bless other people with great items that you no longer need or use. Probably the most commonly neglected area is clearing out clothes, so let's start there. It's amazing and, at times, amusing, to listen to our own rationale for holding on to clothes that we haven't worn in years. We're going to lose weight, it's our favourite sweater (even though we haven't worn it for several years) and other creative excuses.

This time around, instead of taking everything out and putting it all back, ask yourself what's worth keeping and why. Why am I holding on to this? When did I last wear it? Unless you have a very good reason, put it in the 'disposal' pile, not back in the wardrobe or drawer. As a secondary check on yourself, you could add in a proviso that, unless you wear it again three times in the next month, it goes. Now, of course, the more contrary among us will immediately ensure that they do just that, if only to show that they're not hoarding for the sake of it. That's fine: you'll either find that you'd forgotten how much you like the particular garment and keep on using it, or you'll (hopefully) have the honesty to admit to yourself that you really *don't* like it any longer and show it the red card.

It's also a good strategy to plan the whole exercise in full. Don't simply go through things and make piles of items to go at some point; plan it out so that you actually take them straight away to the charity shop, or wherever you've planned. Then it's 'job done', rather than one step, which, if you don't follow through to completion, will simply create more chaos rather than less and probably, in time, find its way back into the cupboard from whence it came.

The same goes with household items. Make a strategic plan so that you are as efficient as possible in not simply identifying what you want to 'lose', but how you're going to do that. Something you no longer need may be just what someone else is looking for, so it's worth putting out feelers before taking other steps, whether it's on a family or friends' WhatsApp group, in community forums, or charities, such as British Heart Foundation, Salvation Army, etc.

Whatever works for you, do it! What we're talking about here is to build into your lifestyle regular slots where you take stock, decide if there are things you no longer need and deal with them. It doesn't have to be often, but it should be regular. For example, with clothes, you could do this a couple of times a year as the seasons change – go through summer clothes in winter and vice versa. If you live in a mansion, of course, you won't have problems with surplus, but most of us land up moving things from one place to another and back again because we simply don't have room.

What about photos?! With the advent of smartphones, taking photos has become a national pastime. It's wonderful to be able to catch the moment, but be honest, how many hundreds of photos do you have stored on your phone, tablet or computer that you've *never* looked at again, and aren't likely to start now! Do you actually need 28 split second versions of the same moment? And do you *really* need to take a photo of every meal you eat?! Choosing your favourite and deleting the rest would be a good place to start.

And really, what's the point of simply keeping them all on your phone? Or even in the cloud? There are easy options now to create photobooks or digital albums which you can enjoy yourself, or share with others.

It may be that you (like me) have landed up with family photos from previous generations. Rather than just throwing them away, or leaving them in a box to be thrown away by someone else, how about scanning them and putting together an album that could be passed on to future generations? People are, by and large, fascinated by their family's history, but we often wake up to this when it's too late – there's no one left who remembers who all these people are and how they connect. Now, that could be a fun and rewarding project, couldn't it?

We looked earlier at the importance of ensuring that special items which you want to go to certain people are clearly earmarked so that they will get to the destination you intend, as well as those things that are of sentimental, rather than monetary value. Check that out again (Chapter Four, 'Personal items') and see what you think.

I'm not saying that it's wrong to have around us things that aren't necessarily of practical use. You may well have items that are precious to you, such as letters, cards, journals, diaries, or whatever. Some of these may be deeply personal; they mean a lot to you, but you wouldn't want others reading them. Well then – be prepared. Make sure that you give your executors and/or family clear instructions about disposing of them.

I have items which aren't highly confidential but mean a lot to me, and I enjoy going through them from time to time, so I've made a 'sentimental mish-mash' box to keep them in. It doesn't have to be elaborate; I simply covered a handy box with pretty wrapping paper. When the time comes, my executors will know that they don't even need to look in the box — they can simply burn it all. I wouldn't mind if they did go through it, but there's more than enough for executors to wade through and this could save them some time.

For the parents (probably mums!) among you, what about all those mementos you've kept from your children's early years? The birth congratulation cards, first shoes, pictures they drew; I'm sure you can add to this list. Maybe you've kept them with the thought that they'd love to have them one day. Are you sure? Or are these *your* memories which, apart maybe from a nostalgic look at them, your now adult children have no desire to keep? More items, perhaps, for that 'sentimental mish-mash' box?

Before moving on, a question — how 'dangerous' is your home? You may think that's a strange question in this context, but I'm thinking of lofts, cellars, garages and sheds — those convenient places where we can just shove stuff out of sight, and rapidly out of mind too. I count myself blessed to be lacking in this area; with no such convenient 'hidey-holes', I can't take advantage of this mixed blessing! However, I know of plenty who have and understand the temptation. It may be that we don't have the time or inclination right now to go through things and make decisions, or that we simply don't want to bite the bullet. We don't really want to get rid of stuff accumulated over many years that carries with it sentimentality, memories, the 'might come in useful' syndrome... you know who you are! So, please, decide that you're going to face it head on, enjoy going through it all and be done with it. If something has been out of sight for more than six months, it's a likely candidate for recycling or disposal. If it's been stored away for more than a couple of years, it almost certainly is. Alternatively, it needs to be taken out and used!

Now that your creative juices have hopefully started to flow, how else might you make sure that life continues as seamlessly as possible for your nearest and dearest? For example, are you the one in your family who does all the cooking? Teach your other half and/or the kids simple recipes they can use. Are you the one who handles all the household affairs? Make sure they at least have a clue about what's where and how things work. That could cover anything from accounts and paying the bills, to using the washing machine, or what to do when the lights go out or the pipes burst!

While we're looking at all this in the context of 'helpful preparations', don't just park it in the 'end of life' box. A regular audit of your life and habits can be life-changing in ways you may not think of. Living lightly, without physical, mental or emotional clutter – is that possible? Yes, absolutely. Some of it may take time to establish (especially if you've developed bad habits!), but the first time around is the toughest.

Once you have established a pattern and rhythm that works for you, it's just a case of regular check-ups to keep it all in order. And then, you can really party!!

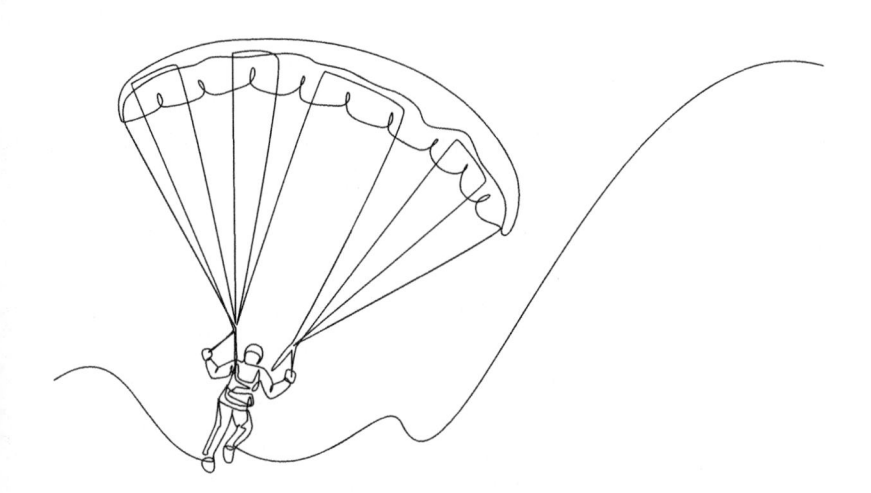

To think about

Bite-sized chunks are the key, especially when it comes to your life data! Don't look at the whole picture and give up before you start. Make a cup of your favourite brew (probably best not alcoholic!), take a good look at your life against the benchmarks we've just talked about and work out what needs to be done and prioritise them.

Get those creative juices flowing because, believe it or not, a lot of this can be fun and hugely therapeutic! Rather than coming up with 1001 great excuses for not doing things, outwit yourself and come up with strategies to overcome your own excuses and possible procrastination!

NOTES FROM THIS CHAPTER

8 DEALING WITH THE INEVITABLE

Finding treasure in unexpected places

> *"The bitterest tears shed over graves are for words left unsaid and deeds left undone."*
> —Harriet Beecher Stowe

At various points in our lives, we are all unavoidably faced with the reality of death. Sadly, there will be times when this is the death of someone very dear to us whether family or friend, and at others we're perhaps a step or two removed from that most intimate circle. And inevitably, of course, it will one day be our own demise approaching!

We'll get to looking at the practicalities that have to be dealt with when someone dies, but I'd like to reflect first on the thorny subject of dealing with the inevitable when everything in us wants to run as fast as possible in the opposite direction. How do we handle things when we know that someone we love (or even ourself) is approaching the end of their life? I think it's probably fair to say that most of us just stoically go through such times, somehow managing, but barely coping.

My personal view is that most Brits are really bad at dying! We're great at travelling together through other life milestones – educational/career success, marriage, pregnancies, etc. With news of a baby expected, there's huge excitement and anticipation, celebrations, baby showers, gifts and the roof really comes off when the little one arrives – more celebrations, gifts and special ceremonies. Now, I'm obviously not suggesting that, when it's the other end of life, we celebrate and party our way towards death, especially when it's someone we really love and care for, although if they're a person of deep faith they may feel there *is* much to celebrate. Does that mean it's wrong to grieve? Of course not. While we can indeed celebrate together, it's natural too for us to feel sad, maybe heartbroken. What I *am* saying is that this terrible and tough road can prove to be a rich and profoundly rewarding experience, resulting in an unexpectedly beautiful way to bring our earthly journey together to a close

I've often thought what a privilege and special joy it is to be present at a birth and I feel the same way about death. Take courage and think about it. Knowing that a life journey is approaching its end is often such a painful time. We all know that this is where we're at, but no one wants to talk about it, so we all pretend it's going to be okay. How sad is that? I really hope that, when it's my turn, I can spend as much time as possible with the people I love – talking, remembering, laughing, crying. And there's the rub! We so often avoid talking about anything emotive because we might cry and that would be terrible. Really? Why do we think that crying together is to be avoided at all costs? We don't pull back from talking together in case we laugh, do we, and there's plenty of research available confirming that crying is just as healthy and healing as laughter.

I'm not suggesting this as a formula, some sort of roadmap of how to deal with death. Different circumstances will, of course, affect the journey in many ways. I'm just recalling the loss of some of my own very dear ones where, subsequently, I've wished that we'd said more. Times when I held back – as did the loved one concerned – both not wanting to upset each other. The sad truth is that you can't do it later, so take courage and join me in thinking about this season of life, one that is as important and potentially amazing as the rest.

Even if you've been excellent at keeping relationships sweet and in good order, what a glorious opportunity to reiterate what you feel. To tell people how much you love them and how wonderful they are. To thank each other, relive and laugh or cry over those memories. It's an opportunity to be honest about your feelings. Maybe you're scared about 'what's next?' and this would be a good opportunity to face that, to explore your own beliefs, read books, talk to someone… whatever helps you find peace. Conversely, it may be that you have no doubts on that score and want to both give reassurance and share your own faith in that regard. It may simply be ensuring that your thoughts and wishes are known, or giving/receiving reassurance that, yes, they are and they will be fulfilled.

Whatever the situation, such a journey is an amazing opportunity to say a proper goodbye with thanksgiving in your heart, along with the sadness. You may think that this is several steps too far and you have no idea about what's next. Nevertheless, many will testify that when you have the privilege of time together, however poignant or difficult it may be, the lasting rewards for those left behind are priceless.

You may well be saying that's all very well, but what about situations where there isn't the luxury of time, where death is sudden and unexpected? That, clearly, is difficult beyond words, whatever the situation, even worse if our last interaction was bad. That's why it's so profoundly important that we live and love well. Then, even with the hardest and worst of circumstances, we can, in time, be comforted that the ground between us was clear and our grief doesn't have to include regret for things said in anger, or that love and appreciation were never expressed.

That's a lot to think about! Maybe it's time for some reflection and soul-searching before moving on to practicalities. Use the journal pages to note down those things that come to mind for further thought and practical action.

Of course, it doesn't stop there, does it, particularly if you're an executor with the responsibility of handling the administration of an estate. How do we get through dealing with practicalities when we're grieving? Handling things with regard to a close relative or friend is a tough call, and it often feels like there's no time to breathe; it's all got to be done yesterday. Some people just want to get everything 'done and dusted', while others don't even want to begin to think about it right now. And, when those who have been given the responsibility for handling things includes people from both extremes, life can become fraught, to say the least.

A good place to start, if you've been appointed as an executor of someone's estate, is to educate yourself now about what will be required and when, rather than panicking when it becomes reality. With an understanding of what needs to be done and when, you can work through it all in an orderly and sensitive way, especially if there's family involved who aren't executors.

A summary of the steps required follows, but you can find more details on any of the following very good and clear websites, which will also be up to date with current legislation. Just enter 'what to do when someone dies' in their search space. A gentle reminder – this summary and these websites all relate to the UK, so if you live elsewhere, please check your own nation's processes.

What to do when someone dies: step by step -
GOV.UK (gov.uk)

What to do when someone dies –
Money Helper (moneyhelper.org.uk)

What to do after a death –
Citizens Advice (citizensadvice.org.uk)

What to do when someone dies –
Which? (which.co.uk)

What to do when someone dies – first steps

1. Register the death within five days.

2. Arrange the funeral – it's important to check if the person who has died had made arrangements for their funeral, which could include prepaid funeral plans or life insurance, burial/cremation wishes/arrangements, etc.

3. Tell the government about the death – use the 'Tell Us Once' service which allows you to inform all the relevant government departments when someone dies. The registrar who deals with the registration of death will explain this to you and either complete it with you, or give you a unique reference number so you can do it yourself, either online or by phone. You must use this service within 84 days of getting your unique reference number. Please note – this service is not available in Northern Ireland.

4. Check if you can get bereavement benefits, i.e. Bereavement Support Payment if your spouse or civil partner has died, or Guardian's Allowance if you're raising a child whose parents have died.

5. Deal with your own benefits, pension and taxes – these may change depending on your relationship with the person who died.

6. Check if you need to apply to stay in the UK – if your right to live in the UK depends on your relationship with someone who died, you might need to apply for a new visa.

7. Deal with their estate – this can be done directly by the person(s) appointed as executor, although there are some situations where you will be wise to use an expert. Probate specialists might be solicitors or accountants and there will be a fee for doing this, which will come out of the estate. However, if the estate is not straightforward, it will save time and headache (and quite possibly also money) to use a specialist.

You might want to think about using a probate specialist if:

- The value of the estate is over the inheritance tax threshold and the estate is still earning a regular income where there are complicated taxes due. The GOV.UK website will have further information on inheritance tax, including the current threshold.
- The deceased died without a will and it's a complicated estate to administer.
- There are doubts about the validity of the will.
- The deceased had dependants who were deliberately left out of the will, but who might want to make a claim on the estate.
- The estate has complex arrangements, such as assets held in a trust.

- The estate is, or may be, bankrupt (also known as insolvent).
- The estate includes foreign property or foreign assets.
- The deceased resided outside of the UK for tax purposes.

Okay – take a breath! It is a lot to take in, so you can see why I suggest that, if you know that you've been appointed as an executor, it would be good to get familiar with things before it's required.

Equally, let's think about those who will have to do this on your behalf. What will your executors or attorneys need to know and what can you do now to make their tasks easier? Hopefully, the above helps to confirm the relevance of all the earlier information regarding making a will, appointing guardians for minor children, etc. and also of compiling your life data bank – in whatever form. Attorneys won't, of course, need to know about your will, but they certainly will need to know how to access the practical details of your life and where important documents are kept. Your executors definitely will need to know the whereabouts of your will and any specific wishes you have regarding funeral, organ donation, etc., but don't stop there. Go through your will with your executors so that they know what it contains and are prepared.

As well as dealing with the estate, it's likely that there will be personal items to dispose of and, in some circumstances, maybe a family home and all the contents. That's huge and can be so difficult to handle. It may, in some situations, simply be a chore to be done, but when it comes to clearing and selling a family home it can seem overwhelming, especially if it's where you grew up. Not only is there a lot of 'stuff' to go through and dispose of, but it can be hugely emotional, like ripping up deep roots. So, how can we ease the way?

As discussed earlier, leaving clear directions about specific items and who they're to go to can avoid a whole heap of arguments and bad feeling. I can recall, way back as a child, when an older family member died, and some relatives simply swooped in and helped themselves to items – ornaments and jewellery without any consultation or discussion. It was never challenged, but a lot of hurt and disappointment was caused. It's pretty simple to ensure that your wishes and any promises you've made are clearly recorded and made known or, as suggested earlier, give them away before you die!

I heard of one couple who did a great job in this respect. Having sorted out all their affairs, they gathered the family together and laid it all out; what they had, how they were leaving it, who would have what and so on. This wasn't a discussion forum; it was creating the opportunity to put everyone in the picture at the same time, so all heard and understood. What a great (and brave?) way to negate any potential for misunderstandings and arguments down the line about what was said by whom.

This is especially important if you know that there are some family members who may be tricky. Sad to say, death and potential inheritance can bring out both the best and worst in people, and it can happen quickly and surprisingly. You may expect people to rally round and respect the wishes of the deceased, but it isn't always so; your executors may find themselves having to manage unexpected and awkward situations. At the very least, warn them if you know that problems could arise and think what you might be able to do now to prevent that.

Clearing an entire home can be a mammoth task, but it doesn't all have to be done within a week. Bigger items like furniture and household goods are much easier to deal with; it's the smaller, more personal things that can create dilemmas and, at times, arguments. There's also, I think, a level of feeling bad at disposing of someone's home; it feels a bit callous, doesn't it? But it's not – it has to be done and the previous owner is fine about that!

While you can just grit your teeth and plough through this as quickly as you can, you can also use the opportunity to create a wonderfully healing experience. Start with the big items, such as furniture, and get them moved either to family members who would like them, to auction if the item is of sufficient value, or to charity shops, etc. That will begin to clear the decks. Then maybe move on to household items such as kitchen equipment, household linens etc. It's so easy now to take photos and circulate them quickly around family to see if anyone wants certain items and, again, if no takers, they can be disposed of.

Now you come to the more personal items that may have far more emotional attachments. How about organising a time (day, weekend, or more, if necessary) when the close family can gather together and go through everything, taking time to remember the stories, the people, the special times? Taking time to laugh and cry together; a journey of laughter and tears, which, although costly at the time, somehow brings peace to the heart and gratitude to the soul. Make and take the time to 'finish well', knowing you've done a good job of completing the affairs of someone you all loved (and still do!) while thoroughly celebrating them.

Another word to the wise here. We are all different, and unique, and that applies too when it comes to grieving. We don't all do it the same. You might think there should be a specific formula or timetable that everyone follows, but there simply isn't, added to which, the various relationships of those grieving with the deceased were different. So, be tender with and listen to one another. It may well be that you need to ask the questions that will bring forth the answers you need to listen to.

Don't make assumptions about what will help someone; for example, deciding to get rid of certain items that you think may upset them. We're there to journey *with* that person, not take over and make decisions for them that later they may regret and blame you for, maybe spoiling your relationship permanently.

Life is a journey and death is part of it. Let's learn to do it ALL well, knowing how to both mourn and celebrate; how to build relationships of unconditional love that are strong, transparent, releasing and life-giving. How to live really well in order to finish this part well. 'This part'? Read on for the final piece of the picture. But first…

To think about

If you knew you only had days/weeks to live, how would you respond? Would there be conversations to be had, letters to write, arrangements to be made, unfulfilled dreams to move on? What needs to change in how you're living today that would enable you to face such a scenario with equanimity? To use those last days or weeks to bring a closure that is full of thankfulness, joy and peace – even along with tears.

Think about all the practicalities that will have to be handled by your executor, family, friends. Have all those conversations happened? Is everything in good order? What do you need to put in place now that will ensure an easy path for them?

NOTES FROM THIS CHAPTER

MARJIE SUTTON

9 TO INFINITY AND BEYOND!

Just when you thought it was all over

"Now this is not the end. It is not even the beginning of the end. But it is, perhaps, the end of the beginning."

—Winston Churchill

Maybe you're wondering what more could there be to talk about. Well, just the small matter of eternity! Perhaps you've never really thought about it, or you may have a vague notion that, when you die, you'll move on to a nice 'other world' where you'll hook up with your nearest and dearest and enjoy living in some sort of perpetual holiday, or super retirement. Maybe your immediate response is, 'Stop right there – I don't believe in any of that', and of course, what you believe is your choice. However, I do believe it, as do many others, and I guess here I'm mostly talking to those for whom, like me, faith is the cornerstone, foundation and fullness of life.

If you think it's not for you, feel free to read no further, although, before you go, maybe you should just think again. After all, what do you have to lose by opening your heart to God and asking him, if he's real, to make himself known to you? Nothing at all. Unless, of course, he *is* real, in which case, you'll be missing rather a lot! You may find it helpful to read *The Case for Christ*[2] by Lee Stroebel, an award-winning legal journalist and self-confessed atheist who set out to investigate Jesus for himself and disprove Christianity's claims about him, with surprising results.

For those like me, who share faith as a follower of Jesus, I would love you to continue reading just a little further, as I have things on my heart to share.

We've dealt with our treasures on earth; what about those in heaven? It's easy to get so embroiled in the affairs of life that the eternal gets side-lined; although that's in our heads, it's not reality. We don't enter eternity when we 'die and go to heaven'. Eternity is here and now and we're already living in it. Our relationship with Father, Son and Spirit doesn't begin when we 'get to heaven'; it's here and now. So, what are you doing with it, here and now? How are you using the time God's given to you here on the earth? Psalm 39:4-5 brings a sobering perspective:

'Lord, remind me how brief my time on earth will be.
Remind me that my days are numbered – how fleeting my life is.
You have made my life no longer than the width of my hand.
My entire lifetime is just a moment to you;
At best, each of us is but a breath.'

---

[2] Zondervan (2014)

Goodness, that paints a different picture! It's so easy to compartmentalise our lives; we often talk about 'my spiritual life' as if it's a separate entity in a box all of its own. However, you and I know that isn't the heart of God, who loves us and wants to be integral in every aspect of our lives. What, actually, are we focusing on and giving our time to?

Here's what Jesus said about it (Matthew 6:20-21):

> *'Store your treasures in heaven,*
> *where moths and rust cannot destroy,*
> *and thieves do not break in and steal.*
> *Wherever your treasure is,*
> *there the desires of your heart will also be.'*

What does that all mean? Simply, that how we live here on earth will shape how we live there, in that eternal kingdom. As we've already seen, reviewing and decluttering/streamlining doesn't apply simply to tangible things. Perhaps you need to take time out to really look at these deeper things also. Jesus is talking here about the desires of our hearts being the engine that drives us. What are those things for you, the things you hold closest?

We're not talking about a God who just hands out tasks, treating us like some sort of servants or workforce; he's all about relationship, partnership. He wants us to know him and be known by him, to walk and work with him. He has made each of us unique, put inside of us qualities, gifts, abilities and dreams. We have the amazing gift of life to treasure and steward, and the fearful freedom to use that simply in the context of 'here and now', or with an eternal perspective.

It's not so much about what we do with our lives, but how. Is God in that strange separate 'spiritual life' compartment, or flowing through the heart of everything you do and are?

In the prayer of Jesus in John 17, he says to his Father, '*I brought glory to you here on earth by completing the work you gave me to do*.' What an amazing thing to be able to say and what questions it triggers.

- Am I pleasing God?
- Am I doing what God called me to do?
- Will I finish it?

Look again at John 17:4 – '*Father, I brought glory to you here on earth by completing the work you gave me to do*'. I love the way Landa Cope writes about this in her book, *The Old Testament Template*[3]:

> '... *Another thing that strikes me in this text is that the Father was glorified because Jesus finished his job... God is not looking at the past, he is looking at the finish. He is challenging me not only to begin well but to finish well. Then, and only then, will he be glorified in my life and through my work. These are sobering challenges and good questions to raise in prayer on a regular basis.*
>
> *Am I doing what God called me to do? Will I finish it?*'

---

3   *An Introduction to The Old Testament Template*, YWAM (2011)

MARJIE SUTTON

NOTES FROM THIS CHAPTER

MARJIE SUTTON

APPENDIX

THE EXTRAORDINARY POWER OF FORGIVENESS[4]
youtu.be/JQ-j7NuhDEY

Hello there, my name is Dr. Andy Knox and I'm going to talk in this vlog today about a subject that is not easy and can stir up a whole host of different emotions. But, what I want to talk about is the extraordinary power of forgiveness.

There are many times people come and see me as a GP with physical pain, with mental health problems and, when we try and explore and uncover what the reasons are behind the things that those people are experiencing, we don't always find a particularly easy answer.

I remember, maybe four or five years ago, this guy came to see me with the most horrendous back pain and I examined him very thoroughly and couldn't really find a reason for the severity of his pain. I couldn't really find anything that would explain the kind of shooting pains that he was getting. So, I sent him for an MRI scan and that was completely normal. So, we tried him on a host of different stretches, we tried him with physio, we tried him with deep tissue massage. We tried him with various different painkillers, getting right up to some

---

4 Andy Knox © 2017, reprinted with permission.

extremely strong stuff, and nothing really touched the pain or made any difference at all. And he was getting very fed up and I was feeling inadequate, to be honest.

So, I went back over the story with him and I said to him, "Listen, can you remember when this pain started, if you had to try and understand what the root was to this pain?" Because sometimes physical pain is a manifestation of deeper emotional pain that we might be feeling. And he said, "I know exactly what caused this pain, but I don't want to face up to it." I said, "Well, so would you rather live with the pain?" and he said, "No, no, no, no. But what caused this pain is just too difficult for me." And he went on to tell me about how his wife had an affair and it had absolutely crushed and broken his world and he'd lost everything, and he'd felt so angry and so bitter and so resentful. He knew that was the very point at which the pain started.

So, I said to him, "Well, medicine is complicated and it's not always very straightforward, and sometimes there's a spiritual aspect to health that can explain some of the physical stuff that we go through. It's not something we're very comfortable talking about in the west, but the Maori people in New Zealand have no problem talking about this, and most of the eastern nations have no problem talking about this either." And so he said, "Well, I don't know if I can forgive her for what she did." and I said, "Well, do you feel that you can live with the pain?" and he said, "No, I don't feel I can live with the pain." I said, "So, how about *trying* to forgive and let it go?"

And I watched him make an incredibly brave and difficult decision to do that, to face up to his pain and to hold it for what it was; to recognize all the difficulties it had caused him and then to forgive. That guy walked back into my room a week or so later with no pain in his back at all.

A couple of years ago, in January, a lady came to see me after a Christmas break and she said, "Andy, I know why I'm depressed." I said, "Why is that?" and she said, "Well, ever since the age of nine, I watched my dad beat my brother every day, as an alcoholic, and I felt so angry towards him and so resentful of him that I know that's the root cause of why I feel so down. But, I've never ever been able to forgive him or had any respect for my father." And she said, "...and I think that's partly what causes the tiredness within my MS; I haven't been able to clean a room in my house for over five years." I said, "Wow, that sounds like a really important revelation for you." And she said, "Yeah, it's been huge. I don't feel like I need my antidepressants anymore." And I said. "So, if it's possible that your depression and part of your MS has its roots in this feeling that you've carried around for a long time, do you think it might be possible to forgive your dad?" and she said, "No, there's no way I will ever forgive that man."

I said, "But, what if it meant that, by doing so, that you yourself could be more free, and you could be more well?" and she said, "Then I suppose I'll forgive him. But I don't know how." So, we talked through a process that I'm going to go on to in my next vlog about how you actually can work through forgiveness. But, she worked that through and she came back and she was like a different person and she said to me, "Do you know what? I've got so much energy. I clean my house from top to bottom; I feel like a whole weight has been lifted off my shoulders and I feel like I can become a light." That's an amazing statement. She's one of my favourite people to have a consultation with; I feel like I get more healed when I see her than when she sees - you know, than anything she gets from me.

Forgiveness is not saying that what happened is okay. Forgiveness is not saying that what happened was just to be forgotten about. Forgiveness is an incredibly brave, gutsy, difficult choice. It's not this lovely emotion that you feel; it is facing up to the full horror of what happened, the upset, the appalling negative consequences that are hard on you and being able to draw a line and say "no more". The consequence of not forgiving can sometimes be more severe; that bitterness, that resentment which twists inside of us might be the root to some of the physical pain that you carry, or some of the mental illness that you have. What if, by forgiving, you could be more free, that you could be more well and that, actually, in doing so, you might set that other person free also.

One of the things our society needs more than anything is forgiveness. And look at its power. Look at the amazing work of the prime minister in Canada, Justin Trudeau, as he's working through age-old generational hurt. Look at the incredible healing that has taken place in Rwanda. Look at Mothers Against Violence in Leeds and Manchester. When we consider the kind of conflicts we still see in Israel and Palestine, in Syria, in Iraq, in Libya - what hope do we have without forgiveness? Without the ability to face up to these appalling atrocities, the things that we have done to one another, unless we're willing to draw a line, say "no more", forgive, and find a different kind of future?

Forgiveness is possible because of this amazing thing called grace. Grace doesn't demand retribution. It faces the fact that no punishment is going to make right the wrong that was caused. Forgiveness sets us and others free and I would invite you to explore whether there is unforgiveness, resentment and bitterness that you carry that might be a root to some of the illness you have. Wouldn't it be great if we were more well? I believe part of that is being able to be people who forgive. In doing so, we set ourselves and other people free. It's really hard and, in my next vlog, I'm going to talk about how we go about forgiving.

HOW TO FORGIVE[5]
youtu.be/EtexaUCBI5k

Hello there. I am Dr Andy Knox and in my last vlog I was talking about the extraordinary power of forgiveness. A lot of people who I work with say to me, *"Okay, I think forgiveness would be a really good thing for me to do. It's not going to be easy, but I don't know how."* So, there is a foundation called the "More to Life Foundation" who do some great work. You can check out their website, you can go on some of their courses, if you feel that would be helpful for you. But they do this process called "the forgiveness process", which is really beautiful and actually takes you through just a series of steps that helps you face up to deal with what's happened and let go.

Now, you can use this process in lots of different ways, so it's very flexible and it even works to do it imagining forgiving someone who may have already, sadly, passed away. You can do it with someone one-on-one, or you can even do it in the mirror. You know, a lot of the times when we struggle to forgive, the person we struggled to forgive the most is ourselves. Sometimes, we carry around incredible amounts of guilt and shame and none of that is good for our health. And sometimes, looking in a mirror and using this process can be absolutely incredible.

So, listen, this is how it goes. The first thing you have to do in the forgiveness process is visualise the person that you need to

---

5   Andy Knox © 2017, reprinted with permission.

forgive. So, if that person - if you can't do it face-to-face, just set a chair down in front of you and sit with that chair, and then imagine that you are talking to that person. Or, sit the person down themselves and say, *"Listen, there's some stuff I need to talk to you about."* Visualize that person, look them in the eyes if you can, or at least have them in the same room as you. Or, if it's yourself, just look in a mirror, look yourself in the eyes and go through this process.

The second part is all about vocalisation, it's about saying the stuff you need to say and the first thing is this statement: *"I have been resenting you for ***."* So, it is not *"You have made me feel..."*, because, whether we like it or not, the truth is that each of us are responsible for our own feelings, for our own responses. No one actually makes us do anything, so this is about saying, *"I have been resenting you for ***"* and whatever it is...

> *I have been resenting you for the way that you spoke to me*
> *I have been resenting you for the fact that you had an affair*
> *I have been resenting you for all the hurt and the pain you caused me*
> *I've been resenting you that you never told me you love me*

Or, you know, whatever it is, whatever that horrendous thing was, *"I have been resenting you for the fact that you abused me."* I have been - whatever those things are, however painful they are, stating them and saying them out loud, I have been resenting you for this. And then you say, *"The benefit to me of holding on to my resentment has been ***."* You see, a difficult truth is that, actually, if we didn't get something out of holding on to our bitterness our resentment, our anger, we wouldn't hold on to it. So, we might say things like

> "The benefit I have drawn from holding on to my resentment has been that it has allowed me to feel superior to you"; or,
> "...it has justified the anger that I have felt", or
> "...it has been the way that I have had some sense of power over you."

Or there might be, you know, loads of different reasons why we hold/have held on to that resentment or that anger. And then we go on to say, *"...but the cost to me of holding on that resentment has been ***",* and there will be lots of different costs of the consequences of not having forgiven. It might be that we've not been able to form really good relationships with other people. It might be that we've just felt angry, or depressed, or anxious, or we've got physical pain. Or there could... I don't want to put words into your mouth. I want to give you examples of the kind of costs that we bear of holding on to bitterness and unforgiveness.

And then, we're going to say, perhaps, some of the toughest words you might ever say. You're actually going to ask that person to forgive you, and it's literally just saying *"Please forgive me."* And you might say *"for ***",* and you might say what those things are.

So, I was working with a couple recently and one of the things we talked about together was *"please forgive me for the fact that I maybe didn't invest as much into you, or make you feel as important as I could have done."* That's not excusing the fact that their partner had an affair, it's just saying that, you know what? I'm sorry too. And sometimes stuff happened that we were completely an innocent victim in something and what happened to us was completely horrendous and awful. A lot of stuff happens to us in childhood. But, even then, we can say *"Please forgive me that it has taken me until now to forgive you, or to come to this place."* Or, *"Forgive me that I felt so angry for so long."*

And then the last one is maybe the three bravest, boldest, but most beautiful words in the English language: *"I forgive you."* Not necessarily an emotional response; a deep, gutsy, bold and brilliant choice: *"I forgive you. I let this go. I draw a line. I say enough is enough, I forgive you."*

And that's the process, and you may have to do it a number of times. You may find that it begins to stir up other issues and you have to go back to that person, or you have to revisit the issue in your mind. Sometimes, we have to keep forgiving many, many times, but it is the start of a process that begins to set you free. That allows lots of forgiveness to flow your way and allows you to be more healthy and well in every dimension of your life. You really can forgive and it really can set you free.

Dr Andy Knox

ABOUT THE AUTHOR

MARJIE SUTTON is a down-to-earth, practical woman who enjoys bringing order into chaos, both personal and corporate. She is a master implementer whose first book, *Vision Accomplished*, shared insights on the working dynamic of visionaries and implementers, drawn from many years of experience. Her work has taken her all over the world, but always back to her roots in southeast London, and her beloved extended family.

Get in touch
Find out more about
Living to Finish Well by visiting
livingtofinishwell.com

Printed in Great Britain
by Amazon